From Midland to Mindanao

From Midland to Mindanao

Reminiscences of the War in the Pacific

James W. Mims

Edited by Claudia Gravier Frigo

With an Introduction by James P. Duffy

State House Press
Buffalo Gap, TX

Library of Congress Cataloging-in-Publication Data

Mims, James W.
From Midland to Mindanao: Reminiscences of the War in the Pacific
p. cm.
Includes Bibliographical references and index.
ISBN 978-1-933337-68-8 (pbk. alk. paper)
ISBN- 1-933337-67-2 (pbk. alk. paper)
1. Philippines World War II 2. Philippines World War II-Biography 3. World War II 4. Texas A&M University

This paper meets the requirements of ANSI/NISO, Z39.48-1992 (permanence of paper)

Binding materials have been chosen for durability
I. Title.
"Cataloging-in-Publication Data available from the Library of Congress"

Manufactured in the United States

First Printing

State House Press
Abilene, Texas

Printed in the United States of America
Distributed by Texas A&M University Press Consortium
800-826-8911
www.tamupress.com

ISBN-13: 978-1-933337-68-8
ISBN-10: 1933337-67-2
Book Design by Rosenbohm Graphic Design

Dedicated to all the soldiers who served with the 24th Infantry Division and their familes

Contents

A Chance Encounter

In fall 2014, I accepted an invitation to speak to a civic group in Midland, Texas. I drove the two hours from Abilene to the capital of the Texas "Petroplex," and finding my way to the meeting venue, enjoyed the catered barbecue lunch and the table banter that comes with these events. By the time all of the business meeting and announcement agenda had been addressed, I was left with a mere handful of minutes to present my topic, the Comanche Empire. I did my best with the time available, and then the meeting dispersed.

I made one connection that day. One of the members introduced me to James Mims, explaining that he had served in World War II. After the meeting, I followed Mims back to his house to take a look at his wartime letters and scrapbook. That was the genesis of this book.

What attracted my attention immediately were his cartoons. As an illustrator for the Texas A&M campus newspaper, *The Battalion*, he honed his power of observation and humor, which he brought with him when he went to war. Other artists—Bill Mauldin and his "Willie and Joe" come to mind—have chronicled the foxhole view of the war with a national audience in mind. Mims doodled for the benefit of him and his family, a more specific and personal vantage point to be sure. Although Mauldin *may* have experienced what he sketched, there is no doubt of Mims's participation in the cartoons he penned.

Then, there were the letters. They told a lot without many specifics—the censors had seen to that. Still, they provided a framework that he then fleshed out with his memoir of those days and those events. Taken together, the reader can see the "see Mom and Dad, this isn't so bad" view that military officials insisted on, now married to the wonder, occasional horror, and reflection of the soldier-turned-citizen of Mims's later years.

Which brings me to the real magic of this work. Mims understood, even at that early age, that he was in the heart of history. Even as we spoke, this man of older than ninety years became animated when he recounted the massive armada assembled in the middle of the trackless Pacific to invade Leyte. He could still feel the salt spray aboard the PT boat as it jolted its way toward a hoped-for, and aborted, rendezvous with fried chicken. He was not one of the first on the beaches, nor was he in a rifle platoon crossing bayonets with fanatic soldiers of the Japanese Emperor, but as his letters and memoir reveal he was a young American on the adventure of a lifetime. He saw the country, and he saw much of the world. The young man of 1944 animated the eyes of this venerable Midland stalwart, and he was again in awe of the history he had helped make.

He did not ask me to publish his words. He had penned them for his family. He has assembled his story so his kids, and their kids, would never forget that, one time a long time ago, he helped win a war in a far-off and exotic land for the good of the country. He was much too modest for self-promotion. Yet, James consented to have his letters and memoirs published if I thought anyone would be interested.

I believe they will be.

Donald S. Frazier

Foreword

Few things transformed the United States like World War II did. Life before and life after do not resemble each other even slightly. As a historian, these things I state as facts. However, as an editor—a critical reader—of history, it is often difficult to find a story that is powerful enough to keep me engrossed, to keep me wondering what happens next, and to keep me wanting to share it with others.

But then I'd never encountered a story—a true history—like that of James W. Mims.

Recruited by State House Press to edit Mims's binder of letters, cartoons, photographs, and remembrances, I accepted without hesitation. Before my first meeting with Mr. Mims, however, doubts creeped into my thoughts. On the drive to Midland, I pored over his binder, trying to calm the inner voice that said I was too inexperienced to handle a project of this magnitude. Further, I worried that he might think I was too young to help tell his story. If he ever felt it, he surely didn't show it.

Over the course of the ensuing months, I worked to capture the essence of his story. At times, we'd communicate via e-mail, and others, we'd talk on the phone. Each time, he easily recalled events and people from the time period; he joked about his naiveté; and even proved to be an expert—through research on his unit and division—that properly placed himself in the "big picture" during World War II.

I've tried to keep in mind what I learned from our meeting and our conversations as this book took form. The year is 1943 and a young man from West Texas, devoted to his family, finds himself far from home, which is the only place he really wants to be. And how that young man finds his voice through weekly, and sometimes, daily letters home accompanied by cartoons and photographs to a world so far removed from his upbringing.

Sifting through the realia of Mr. Mims's life during World War II proved to be a daunting task. I considered and reconsidered each piece carefully; I made decisions about what to edit out and what to keep in. What I crafted—as any editor hopes—is a snapshot of Mims's journey across the United States and the world, taking the reader along for the journey. Puzzling the pieces together to "create" the story you are about to embark on—a story he only ever intended for his children and grandchildren—I found myself speechless at times, laughing loudly at others, and ultimately, as I reached the end, crying because the story was over.

It's taken me several weeks to sit down and write this because ultimately I knew that this is when my "job" was done, the final piece of project in its place. Truthfully, I've delayed writing it, wanting my time with Mr. Mims—as a young soldier or an older gentleman—to go on and on. I hope you find his story as fascinating as I have because it and its author have left an indelible mark on my soul.

Claudia Graver Frigo

Introduction

Many historians who favored the war in Europe to garner more interest have long sidelined the war in the Pacific, especially the southwest Pacific. In the last few years, a limited but growing number of books have appeared dealing with places such as New Guinea, the Philippines, and the Solomon Islands. Now comes a volume explaining what it was like on the ground, or rather, in the mud in some of these places.

When James Mims left the classrooms at Texas A&M and entered the U.S. Army in January 1943, he expected that his two years in Field Artillery ROTC would result in his assignment to an artillery unit. That was when he got his first lesson on how the Army operates; he was assigned to the combat engineers. By the time his troop ship sailed under the Golden Gate Bridge in June 1944, Mims was a Sergeant in a Photo Interpretation unit.

The world Mims was sailing to was radically different from anything he had ever known. Described by veterans and historians alike as one of the worst places on earth in which to fight a war, the island of New Guinea was covered in deep jungle and swamps that harbored a variety of animals and insects that as was threatening to a soldier's life as the Japanese enemy. New Guinea was where General Douglas MacArthur, Commander-in-Chief of the southwest Pacific Theatre selected to halt the Japanese advance against Australia. From there he would lead his several hundred thousand American and Australian troops leap-frogging along the large island's coast leading to the Philippines.

Mims relates the difficulty of life in this environment, but he never loses sight of the importance of the work he was performing. He describes sailing from Hollandia, New Guinea, aboard the USS *John S. Land* heading for the invasion beaches at Leyte in the Philippines. The Naval Transport was more than six hundred ships assembled for the invasion. Its passengers included the Philippine President, Sergio Osmena and his staff.

We accompany Mims as he climbs down the ship's rope ladder into a landing craft and heads to shore. Later in this collection of letters written home and recollections following the war, Mims describes working with Japanese American soldiers who acted as interpreters for prisoner interrogation and meeting Filipino guerillas who provided them with valuable information on enemy movements. Mims went from Leyte to Mindoro where his unit took up residence on a sugar plantation then on to Mindanao in April 1945, before returning to the United States under tragic circumstances.

Here is a part of war, and of World War II, rarely discussed: no generals, no admirals, just soldiers doing their duty as they struggle to survive.

James P. Duffy
Author, *War at the End of the World*

Remembrances of World War II

These notes are written beginning in 1991, fifty years after the Japanese bombing of Pearl Harbor on December 7, 1941. Human memory is not reliable, but I will set these things down as I remember them now, and leave plenty of room for error!

I have used my letters as the basic documents. The originals of these were saved by my mother, prompted by the fact that her family had saved the letters written by her grandfather, E. G. Littlejohn, during his four-year Civil War combat experience. I made a copy of my letters, supplemented by the explanatory memoranda, for each of my three children.

So there are two stories here: one is in these letters, which really tell almost nothing about where we were and what we were doing; the other is in these notes. I write these to and for my family, primarily, to record my eyewitness view and participation in one of history's unique events: MacArthur's return to the Philippines on October 20, 1944.

Texas A&M, 1941–1942

I was a freshman at Texas A&M when World War II started for us on December 7, 1941. I was in the band and our dorm was No. 11. My room was on the ground floor, and I was studying that Sunday afternoon when students came running across the area hollering that the Japs had bombed Pearl Harbor! Everyone crowded around radios to get the news. At that time, A&M was all military, so it was obvious where we would be headed. The only question was, "How soon?" I vividly remember going into the room of one of our seniors, Claude Stewart, later that evening. He was sitting on his desk with his senior boots on and a most serious and forlorn look on his face. War had suddenly become very real to him. About one third of those young band members were killed during the next few years and many others were wounded.

A&M won the Southwestern Conference in football in 1941 and played in the Cotton Bowl on January 1, 1942. There was a special half-time activity, a ceremony to swear in a group of Navy volunteers, including some ball players. The band stayed on the field through all of this and our horns froze together! It was really cold.

A&M soon had personal involvement in the Pacific War. At this time, Corregidor was the last American stronghold against the Japanese forces in the Philippines. The American artillery commander on Corregidor was General George F. Moore, a 1908 graduate of Texas A&M and A&M Commandant from 1938 to 1940.

Twenty-seven of his besieged garrison identified as Texas Aggies. Under General Moore's leadership, this group, while still on Corregidor, took part in what is probably, the most well-known Aggie Muster ever celebrated. Aggie Muster is a time-honored tradition at Texas A&M that celebrates the camaraderie of the school while remembering the lives of Aggies who have died, specifically those in the past year.

As the Japanese laid siege to the island, despite the fierce fighting and including one 5-hour stretch where an estimated 1.8 million pounds of shells pummeled the island, Moore held a roll call—known as muster in army terms—on April 21, 1942, calling the names of each of the Aggies under his command. . . . Only twelve of the twenty-seven survived the battle and the POW camps to which the survivors were sent.

You can't fight a war without calesthenics! Apparently whichever side can do the most exercises wins! One of our first changes was to get up an hour earlier (daylight savings time) for this activity. We also went on a year-round schedule. We had a week off after school was out in May and started the next school year, the summer 1941. During that summer, Hollywood came to A&M to make *We've Never Been Licked*. It was fun watching the filming, and the band was in many of the scenes. I did not see the film until some months later after I had entered the army and was stationed in Boston. It was great to see all the familiar scenes, and many friends in the pictures, but it heightened the homesickness a lot!

We had a member of our class named Wallace who flunked out, joined the Air Corps, got his commission, and came back for a visit the fall of 1942. It was decided to play a trick on one of the "frogs," a fellow named Vane in the Infantry Band. He was told that Lt. Wallace was on a special G-2 mission to catch a spy at A&M who was sending code signals to the enemy. The plan was for Vane to be sent to an upper classman's room. Upon entering, he would see the occupant apparently sending Morse code. Lt. Wallace was then supposed to enter, confront the "spy," who would draw a pistol and shoot Wallace, and threaten Vane's life if he said anything. The body of Wallace was to be hauled off by other "spies." There were other refinements to the plan, but things didn't get that far. Instead of being frozen in his tracks, upon seeing the gun, Frog Vane fled . . . straight to the Commandant's office, completely running over Wallace and friends in the process! As one might expect, the report was received with something less than enthusiasm. It took a lot of explaining to get that all smoothed over with the authorities.

I think that it was in the fall of 1942 that we had special visitors to the campus, Ensign Gay (George H. Gay, Jr.) and Col. Hilger (Col. John A. Hilger). These were two of the first aces or heroes of the war. Gay had survived the Battle of Midway, which was probably the turning point in the Pacific War. He had been shot down and watched the battle from the water. He was the only source of accurate information about what all happened. Hilger was, I believe, a Marine. They talked to us about their adventures. Most impressive for a bunch of kids.

Monday Nov. 17, 1941
College Station, Texas

Dear Family,
Well, here I am back from the Corps Trips. It was really lots of fun. A&M is in a fair way to become S.W. Conference champs again--Yippee!!

The reason I am writing this now is that when I answered a fish call Thursday, I tripped and fell down in the hall and sprained my left wrist. As you know I have been punching the bag because I couldn't do gymnastics on account of my knee, and now I sprain my wrist. It is better though now. This is my usual P.E. period that I'm excused for today & Wednesday.

Here is the way my grades came out. A- in Spanish, B in Biology, English, and Military Science, C in Math and History. I should have done better in Math and History, but I just can't seem to pick that History up.

I'm glad to hear that Cormick's up and feeling better. How is Uncle Basil getting along? I guess I'll be seeing him soon. All I want to do is sleep but I know that I won't. Poor Midland football team! I guess they win the cellar this year. I surely hope our team is in good shape so you all can see them play a good game like the S.M.U. one. By the way, we saw Windell in Houston. He is playing some good football for the freshmen down there. That is sure rotten country.

I'm going to have to have my horn fixed. One of the keys has quit working. I believe it needs a new spring. I'll tell you all about that when you come down. You can guess how glad I'll be to see you all. It seems that there was never anything but A&M and yet we have been here such a short time.

I went to the dentists last week and the girl had given me a date for the wrong week so I'll have to go this Wednesday. Don't know yet what will have to be done but I guess it's nothing too bad.

Love to all --
James
P.S. Tell the cat hello!

May 4, 1942
College Station, Texas

Dear Folks,
I got your letter and was glad to hear from you. I am sending you some more Batts and you can get a pretty good line-up of everything. The schedule for the 16th is about as follows: We have a review of about 2 hours or longer Saturday morning and then we turn in our G.I. wool uniforms. Since the band is the last organization to march off, we'll be later than the rest, but we should have plenty of time to get to Waco. I told Tad last night that he would come with us & Ken already knew it. If you intend to see the review, you should be here about 8:30 I guess. I'll let you know the exact time later. Dado is rather expecting you to come by there. Are you still planning to?

I have to register Wednesday for my war rationing book. I'll bring it home when I come I guess. There's only one thing I really want when I come home and that is home-fried-chicken! I might like some tea without sugar, too. They used to let us have our own sugar, but now they just sweeten it all with sacharin before they serve it and I don't like it that way.

The editor of the Batt magazine for this coming year came around to see me the other night and said he wanted me to be Asst. Art Editor this year. The next year I can be Art Editor which draws $10 a month! I think I'll do it if I can.

I talked to my Spanish prof today & he advised me to take a novel course in Spanish this next term to improve my vocabulary before I enter conversation. Junior Spanish is conversation anyway so I'll be better off. I guess that's what I'll do.

I'll see you soon. Tell Uncle Basil and everybody else hello--

Love to all,
James

P.S. Mrs. Brown told me she saw you the other day. Wish I had been with her!

Our View from Dorm 16, Texas A & M

June 1, 1942
College Station, Texas

Dear Folks,
I got my razor etc. today. Much obliged. I knew you'd find them! I thought my razor was in the card-board box, but sure enough, it wasn't.

It is quite warm alright. Ken and I are sitting here with the fan on us. It helps some. We are on the hot side of the dorm, but are going to move in about a week to the other side. The freshman are over there now. We have really been giving them a talking to. They are just as scared and ignorant of what they are expected to do as we were. They just stare with their eyes stuck out and their mouths open:

I still have to buy a couple of books which haven't come in, but I am pretty well fixed otherwise. We got our 2 pr. of G.I. pants and 2 G.I. shirts this morning. The shirts are a little heavy, but I guess they'll have to do.

We got the paper today. Say, can you tell me anything about Tad? I have heard he is missing.

Nothing else to say right now except that I got a haircut! I'll write again before long.

Love to all--
James

June 13, 1942
College Station, Texas

Dear Folks,
I'm pretty well started in my studies now. We've had 5 or 6 daily quizzes and I've done well in all but the Chemistry. I now have another trig teacher. I started last year with Ross, changed to Ponter, started with Koss and now have Grant. Koss would have taught us some trig, but Grant is an old maid fuss budget who is too easy and mamby-pamby and I don't believe I'll learn much under him. George Conly from Midland is in my class. He's one of the Midland fish.

I went up and talked (to) Captain Lerner about changing to the signal corps and then to Col. Boles about my chances for a contract in the Field Art. He said I had (an) 8 out of 10 chance of getting one in the Artillery so I decided to stay in the band. Our military instructor who recommends the cadets for contracts is from Stanton and is a nephew of Ed Dickeuss I've already talked to him several times and he knows my name. Maybe it will help some. He's the same Lt. Sale whose picture the girls have at the studio. By the way, what about asking them to send me some of those pictures we took. Did the color pictures come out pretty well? I'll try to write the girls soon.

I'll write again soon. I got your letter and much obliged for the gum. I wrote Horace Brown and sent him a Batt. Tell all the Kids hello and Uncle Basil and the rest.

Love,
James

College Station, Texas
August 11, 1942

Dear Folks,
Well, it seems like things never stop happening to me! I had an appointment with the dentist yesterday and had 2 teeth filled. He found 2 more that also need filling so I'll have to go back. I can't get an appointment until Sept. 4 though. I made the appointment yesterday last July when I had my teeth cleaned, the bill for which I'm enclosing. Dr. Lawrence said I could just wait and settle it all at once if I wanted to, but you can pay the enclosed bill now if you had rather. Last week I discovered 2 wisdom teeth coming in. Dr. Lawrence saw them yesterday and said he thought they were coming in crooked and to go by the hospital at school to get x-rays made. I did that yesterday afternoon after I left his office. It goes on my medical bill that is already paid. I've felt lousy all day thinking about the Camp meeting and my not being there. I was on rock bottom again after I came back from drill and saw the clock say 5:00, time for the men's meeting.

I struggled over to the hospital and got my x-rays. It was the final blow. Fate had dealt me a dastardly blow when I was down. It was the last straw, so to speak. I was really in the dumps. And besides, my arms are covered with heat rash, and my knee has been giving me trouble also. I guess I'll have to have some teeth pulled soon. Send these negatives back as soon as you can, so I can take them in and show Dr. Lawrence. He wanted to see them. But never say die, is my motto. Laugh at fate's sneering face and struggle on, tasting

Academic Building, Texas A&M, 1941

the bitter dregs of defeat and disappointment. Life may be a bed of roses but they surely are thorny.

I got a letter from Frances Stalen and she said Nell Cowden is to marry in September sometime. Liza wrote sometime back and says that Kathlyn Collins is going to marry. Clayton Upham is already married! Eeek! It makes me feel quite odd. It just doesn't seem that I'm that old. In fact, I'm just waiting to come home so I can play cars again. I guess I'm nuts! (Well, I am!!)

We'll be going through the Commando Course here soon, I imagine. Our freshmen worked on that this afternoon during drill, helping them construct it. I expect that it will be pretty rough.

Tell everybody hello for me and write when you have time. I like to get a little use out of our P.O. box. Really wish I could go to Ruidoso with you--

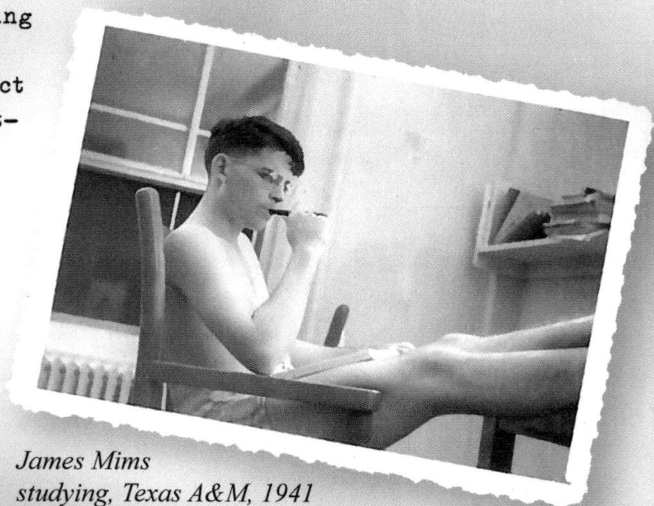

James Mims studying, Texas A&M, 1941

Love to all,
James

October 11, 1942
College Station, Texas

Dear Folks,

That date certainly does look odd. Only one more week! It just doesn't seem right. (P.S. Don't throw my soldiers and trucks away yet! I may get back to them.) If you want to send me something, here's what I would like. I could use one of those desk calendars with a place to write future engagements. I would like a copy of that new book Big Spring. Books of any kind would be well received, and of course anything edible! (Send no scrap metal, though!)

The Field Artillery Ball is going to be next Friday night. Ken may have a date. Bobby Nolan from Midland lives on the 2nd stoop in our dorm. He went some with Gene Ann this past summer and is asking her to come over from Austin. Gene Ann said Helen Armstrong might come with her. Ken will probably get a date with her. I don't know whether to go or not. I have my physics "A" quiz the following Monday. I haven't done a bit of studying since I've been back here. I can't set up to study because I get so sleepy and I can't concentrate. I wished I could get to work or take a couple of weeks vacation in the mountains.

The picture show business may pick up around here soon. There are supposed to be some 75 people from Hollywood here by the 1st. Robert Cummings and Ann Gwynn are going to be the leading characters. I may have a chance to meet them through my high and mighty office as Art Editor! I'm simply thrilled to death!

I had to play at the cavalry house show yesterday afternoon and stayed out there all evening. We listened to the game on a portable radio one of the freshmen had. I sure didn't like the way it came out, but at least it wasn't a Conference game. This school still has a fair record. We'll really have to hustle if we beat T.C.U.

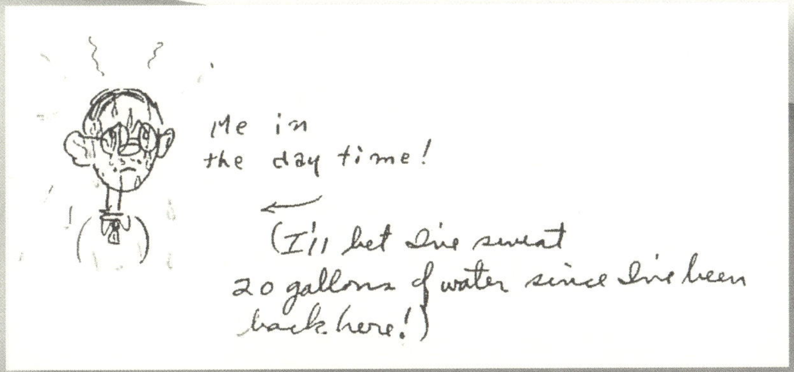

I haven't gotten my Ratarian yet, but I guess it will be here soon. The Batt comes out tomorrow night. I'll send you a copy in a few days. I've got to quit so I can study. There was something else I wanted to tell, but I won't remember until I seal the envelope. I'm sending the papers. Maybe it was in that. Thanks for Billy's address.

Love to all,
James

October 22, 1942
College Station, Texas

Dear Folks,
I got the box last Saturday and it was really fine. I couldn't find a thing wrong with the cake! It <u>was</u> really good. Ken and I finished it up tonight. We still have a part of the cheese left and some of the candy. Just don't feel any different, so I guess I must hold my age well. And I agree with you that I may as well expect one (a birthday) practically every year from now on.

I went to the ball Friday night. It was a pretty good dance, but I knew hardly any of the girls. I haven't danced in so long I've forgotten how. I think Gene Ann and Helen were worn completely out. After the dance on Friday, the game, walking around the campus in high heel shoes, and the Corps dance Saturday night they were pretty well done in. From what Ken said, they both had great big blisters on their feet. Both of the girls seemed to have a good time and liked the school a lot. I guess it is different from the University. Elma Jean and Margaret Ann West were here Saturday for the Corps Dance so there was quite a representation from home.

I would have written sooner, but I have really been busy. Twice last week I was up until 4:00 o'clock. That Accounting really takes the time. I have my "A" quiz today. My Bull Text quiz was Wednesday and my Physics Monday. We won't be so rushed from now on, though. Ben Schleider, the drum major said that the formation for the Arkansas game would probably be the last this year. We aren't going on any Trips. It may be that we'll get a week off Thanksgiving instead of Christmas and have no Christmas holidays. I'll let you know as soon as I know. By the way, what is my draft number?

Write when you can and thanks again for that <u>good(!)</u> cake.

Love,
James

Forts Bliss and Leonard Wood, 1943

In the fall of 1942, the chief aim was to get into the Enlisted Reserve Corps (ERC). The wisdom at that time was that the ERC would stay in school. I couldn't pass the physical. "Why, with those eyes, you'll never even get in the army." (But I did!) So I left school Christmas of 1942 and took voluntary draft in January 1943. As it happened, even those who enlisted in the ERC were called up in March and April and went many and various ways. I entered the army at Fort Bliss, El Paso, Texas, on January 7, 1943. Since I had two years of Field Artillery ROTC, I assumed that that is where I would go. But, no! Since I had taken mechanical drawing in high school, I was sent to the Combat Engineers for basic training at Fort Leonard Wood, Missouri! Thus, the army.

It was cold in El Paso in January 1943. We were quartered in pyramidal tents and slept with everything on that we had. We even got extra mattresses from a nearby tent to use for cover. Induction center was the usual routine of shots, haircuts, uniforms, General Orders, orientation films, and close order drill. J. R. (Buster) Dublin, a lifelong friend, and I had a virulent case of "ROTC"; he from NTAC and I from A & M, so we gave the corporal who was trying to cause us to march a lot of "as you were!" He was not very good. Three other friends from Midland were J. B. Barrington, Bill Truex, and Jesse Moreno. There were so many Orientals around that we wondered if we were in the right army. In due course, Pvt. Mims, 38438243, shipped out for Fort Leonard Wood, Missouri, for Basic Training.

Our train trip took us through Midland to Dallas and then to Neuberg, Missouri, which we reached at 4:00 AM and it was really cold there, 7 degrees below zero! We were trucked to camp, fed breakfast, and then sent to our barracks. Our first project was to assemble some double-deck bunks. Then three of us were sent out to the rock quarry. The sun was shining, but it was bitter cold. The sergeant took pity on me and put me in the little hut used as an office to tend the fire. I got so close to the coal stove that I singed my pants leg, and after several cleanings, the piece just fell out.

Fort Leonard Wood was a tough camp. Our training was infantry style, but also included all of the necessary engineering skills from road and bridge building, to explosives and tank traps. My first duty was pulling targets at the firing range. We were up early, worked hard all day, ate everything in sight, and slept like a log at night. We had an excellent bunch of trainees, mostly from Kentucky. These were fellows who knew how to use tools and weapons, and had I stayed in Engineers, I would have been happy to have been in combat with them. We had good officers and non-coms, too. A Capt. Combs was our company commander, and Sgt. Barber was our platoon sergeant. Our day started early with reveille broadcast from a loud speaker atop a high pole at Battalion HQ, followed by music. We would stand in formation for roll call and be so cold that we wouldn't touch any part of our clothes! Then back to the barracks to make beds, sweep and mop our area, eat breakfast, and fall out for the activity of the day.

Our days were full. Training films, hikes, qualifying with the M1 rifle, erecting a Quonset hut, building trestle bents and bridges, using the gas mask with tear gas, making and using Bangalore torpedoes, stringing barbed wire, and all the necessary training to become soldiers. Perhaps the toughest work was the week at ponton school. Engineers build two kinds of bridges, ponton and pontoon, but mostly ponton. The difference is that a ponton is open and may also serve as a boat, while a pontoon is closed. Ponton school was located on the Big Piney River, which looks as though Huck Finn should come around the bend at any moment. It is on the far side of the Fort and has its own small huts for troops to stay in and its own mess hall. Our job was to learn how to build the various bridges our army used from the Infantry foot bridge to the tank bridges using heavy metal barges for support. This is back-breaking work. For example, one vehicle type bridge uses six-man assault boats. The procedure calls for several men to row across the river dragging a heavy line. The line is attached to a steel cable that must then be dragged across the river and secured to a tree or something similar on the far bank. This becomes the guide to keep the bridge from washing downstream. Then the other boats must be carried to the water, turned over and floated, backed up to one another, secured stern to stern with pins, and this becomes the ponton. Each ponton is secured to the line, balks are attached, and the bridge moves out across the river. All of this is done in assembly line fashion and in combat would probably be done under enemy fire. After each bridge is built, it must be disassembled, everything put up, the area policed, and then it's time to go to chow. We had no trouble sleeping, even though the bunks were just wooden slats!

Three Midland Men Inducted Into Army

FORT BLISS—James R. Dublin III, James W. Mims, and Marse R. Woods, all of Midland, have been inducted into the Army here.

Mims is the son of Mr. and Mrs. Percy Mims, Dublin is the son of Ben W. Dublin and Woods is the son of Mr. and Mrs. John Woods. The inductions were announced by First Lt. Reese Cleveland, public relations officer and former Midland resident.

Sunday

Dear Folks,
Well, things are really fine so far. We got in tired Thursday night, they put us in trucks and hauled us to the induction center at the post, gave us bedding and a meal and put us to bed. We had a fine meal on the train for dinner.

I had a disappointment at the physical that really burned me up. The doc gave my eyes 20-100, 20-200 vision. After we had all our tests, we filed by a Lt. Col's. office to be classified. I told him about the E.R.C. etc., so he told me to get my clothes on & and come back to him, that he was an eye man and would recheck my eyes. I dressed and he checked them. He said that my right eye wasn't even 20-200; it was about 20-175. In other words, I should have passed the E.R.C. exam with flying colors. He gave me a <u>1-A (rejected)</u> classification so I could go back to school & try to get back in, etc. I told him I was too far behind now and since I was this far, I would just go ahead, since they haven't decided what to do with those sophomores at school, yet. So I was accepted.

We got sworn in and got our clothes yesterday morning. The overcoat is really swell as is everything else. You should see us in our fatigue clothes. We got those little steel helmets that fit under the heavy steel ones used in battle, 2 pr. shoes, shirts, underclothes pants, socks, gloves, field jackets, mess kits, etc. Is Dad's mess kit still at home? I may send for it when I'm stationed. My knife, fork, and spoon are allright, but my kit is not in good condition. We were sure cold the first night under 3 blankets. The next night I doubled 2 of them & put the other on top which was much better. Last night I had my long handle underwear and my overcoat on top, I was nearly warm. We have seven in our little hut with one stove and two big ventilators. This is the coldest place. I haven't been warm but about twice. They really feed us, though.

We got our G.I. haircuts yesterday and our heads are really cold. Clippers all around & two inches on top.

Love,
James

Pvt. James W. Mims
U.S. Army
Co. C 1815th Unit
Fort Bliss, Texas

Jan. 13, 1943
Tuesday

Dear Folks,
Well, I'll try to write this so that you can read it. When we got here, I didn't know whether we were in the right army or not. All they seemed to have here were a bunch of Japanese!

They took us through all our processing. We got finished up with everything today. We got our dog tags and small pox and typhoid (shots). We have Battalion detail tomorrow, our first one. We report at 7:30 to clean up the post here at Co. C, including cigarettes, paper, etc. We report again at 1:00.

You should see the clothes they give us here. Canvas leggings, heavy overcoat, fiber helmet, undershorts and shorts, long woolies, field jacket, blouse, canteen, mess kit, shaving and other toilet articles, 2 pr shoes (9 ½ C), wool and khaki shirts and pants, and a khaki and a wool overseas cap. It's really swell. We also have a couple of barracks bags.

I took my tests yesterday and made 139 on my I.Q. They told me at the interview this morning that I had a high aptitude for radio. I told them that my hobby was cartooning and told them that I could type. I ask about officer candidate school and they said I shouldn't have trouble getting most anything I wanted because of my high grade. Buster said they didn't tell him his grade but it is good enough for Officer Candidate School.

We did some drilling this afternoon. It was really a mixed up bunch of draftees. Bill, Buster, and I all have had military, Bill having gone to New Mexico A&M. Some of the men this afternoon were Navaho Indians who couldn't even understand English.

You should see us with all our hair cut off, our fatigue clothes on, and these heavy-soled G.I. shoes. We really look sloppy, but they are really comfortable.

It is really cold here. We sleep in little huts with big ventilators and little stoves.

Love to all,
James

Monday 17, 194(3)
Newburg, Missouri

Dear Folks,
Well, I hope you'll excuse my not phoning when I came threw Midland Sunday morning on that 5:30 train, but I was under govt. orders to make no calls & write no letters. We left El Paso, 10 of us, about 9:30 Saturday night and rode to Ft. Worth. Then north to the state of Missouri. I was wrong about seeing country I had never seen because we

went thru Oklahoma & where ever else we went at night. We got here at Fort Leonard Wood about 5:30 this morning. This is an engineer replacement center and I can't figure why I'm here instead of Fort. Sill or some artillery fort.

I understand I'm classified as a Craftsman, due to my mechanical drawing in high school. I have forgotten a lot of it, but I guess I'll get training if I'm to do that work. It's cold here and there's snow on the ground. I wish I had gone where it's a little warmer. Buster was sent to Lubbock at Sheppard(?) Field, and the other boy in our hut to San Antonio Dental lab. We've been busy inside all day today, the barracks and making beds for new men coming. I guess we'll start drilling tomorrow. I could use some more coat hangers. Be sure to tell George to take some with him. We are in 2-story barracks like the ones at the field at home. It is really nice. I got to see the Evans in El Paso while I was there. I also phoned Mrs. Maluf. She invited me out to her home but I didn't have opportunity to go. I'll write more when I have time.--

Wednesday-
Did I say it was cold? Yesterday morning it was 7 below when we got up! We were on rock quarry detail yesterday. Our barrack bags had not come so I didn't have my wool underwear. They put me in the office to feed the fire so I just brought in a load of wood and sat by the fire all day. I guess I'm just a natural gold-brick. I'm now in the 3rd platoon, Company A, 29th battalion, Engineers Replacement Training center. We had our classification checked this morning and received papers to fill out for Officer's Candidate School. I'll take 13 weeks basic training first, right during the coldest part of the year. My toes aren't warm yet.

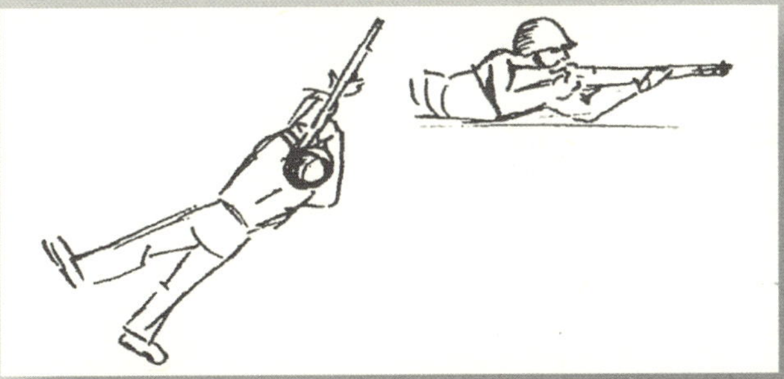

We had our second typhoid and our tetanus shot today. My arm is a little sore. We also got some additional equipment this morning, including a pair of high-top, rubber overshoes. They will be nice to wear in the snow and slush.

Fort Leonard Wood is really a large place. I think there are about 65,000 men here! We are about half way between Springfield and St. Louis, but they are the only places worth going to and about 3 hrs. from here.

When you send the coat hangers, about 8 will do, send me some cardboard, about 6 of those that I have there at home, a bottle of India ink, penstaff, and about 5-- worth of pen points (any size). I bought some and took them home before I left, but I don't know what I did with them.

You'll have to excuse my not sending Dad a present on the 18th, but I've been slightly busy lately. Any how, <u>many happy returns</u>!

I'll write again soon.--

Love,
James

Co. a 29th E.T. Btn (Engineer's Training Battalion)

Saturday 23rd
3rd Platoon
Ft Leonard Wood, Mo.
U.S. Army

I didn't have time to mail the letters so I'll add more on.
We had some foot drill yesterday. The day before, we went to the target range and worked in the pits, sticking the targets up, counting the holes, and then pasting them. We wore overshoes, overcoats, cartridge belts, etc., and did double time out and back. It wouldn't have bothered me except that I had new shoes on and they wore a blister on my heel. It was just to help toughen us up. Those bullets make a very discouraging sound when they whish overhead (and) whack into the target.

We had squad drill this afternoon and we were drilling around when Sgt. Barker, our platoon sgt, said "Mims, do you think you can give these men some drilling?" (I don't know how he knew my name!) I said yes, I could, so he let me drill them awhile. I may get a corporals rating in a few weeks because nearly all of the cadre of Co. A is going to a new camp in Oregon. We would be acting non-coms, but not receive the pay of a corporal. However, I'm not counting my stripes yet.

We have been issued Garand rifles and will start drilling Monday. I don't know anything about rifles, but I dare say I'll learn.

This camp is about 3 hrs. from Springfield and from St. Louis. We are allowed 2 week-end passes during this. 12 weeks training and they run special excursion trips for soldiers to these 2 tours, about $2.75 round trip.

We are eating in (ran out of ink) the mess hall, but are using our mess kits. There are about 100 more men in the company this time than usual and there aren't enough plates. I haven't hit K.P. yet. Never mind sending the mess kit of Dad's but send one wooden coat hanger for my overcoat, please. It is a little heavy for the wire ones.

We got some name tags to sew on our field jackets and overcoats so the non-coms can learn our names sooner.

I think I'm going to like this a lot. It's a lot like school and my training there will help. I wish I wasn't quite so far from home, but here there won't be anything to distract us.

I'll write again soon. I'm pretty well fixed up now, so maybe I'll have a little more time.

Love to all,
James

P.S. I'll try to get pictures if I can. Buster took some at El Paso. You can see Mrs. Dublin about them.

YE OLDE FORTE

Sunday

Dear Family,
There have really been lots of things happening here, so many that I don't know exactly where to begin. I received the box, money, and the letters from you, sister, and Uncle Basil. I also heard from Aunt Mildred, Dado, Mrs. Williams, and Liza. Mrs. Williams also told me about Ken receiving the check in Dallas. I really got a kick out of it. Mrs. Williams said she is sending me a box! I thought that real nice of her. Her address is 4002 Prescott Ave. Dallas.

We started training Monday 2 weeks ago and these past two weeks have really been full. We were issued Garand rifles and have to keep them clean. I can take mine apart and reassemble in the dark, I believe. It is really a fine weapon. Last Sunday we went to the firing range and fired 4 shots to get our sights in line. There are several positions for firing we have to learn. They are rather hard to get into. The sling on the rifle is adjusted around our left arm as tight as is necessary. We fired from a prone position. The hardest thing is getting the left elbow under the gun. We stand facing a little away from the target, legs spread, then drop to a kneeling position, catch our fall with the gun butt, roll over a little and line on the target.

We aimed at the bull's eye and tried for a good grouping. Then we corrected our range. The gun really fires nicely and shoves but doesn't kick like the Springfield. We're going to fire again tomorrow, I think.

We are learning to tie knots. That is one thing Engineers have to know. We'll use lots of them later.

Wednesday is our exercise day. We have calisthenics every morning but we get double dose on Wednesday. They have an embarkation tower which simulates boarding and loading a boat. Then we run an obstacle course. I couldn't make the wall the first week when we had our overcoats on, but it was warmer last Wednesday and with my field jacket on, I made it. The first week we had a hike with combat packs and rifles. A combat pack just contains raincoat & a pair of socks. Last week it had rained on Tuesday and we had full field pack. It was pretty tiring trying to climb these hills, some just like that East Texas mud, others (page cut off) black gummy mud. We only went about 3 miles as the crow flies, but we went another three or four up and down. The weather was pretty, though, so it could have been worse.

They show us lots of training films here, films on close order and extended order drill, gas drill, and some propaganda films about the war. There are seven in the series about "What We Are Fighting For." We have only seen the first but it was very good. It traced the development of the War previous to the fighting now and gave the Japs moving into Manchuria as the beginning of the whole business.

Extended order drill is really rough on the old bones. That is where you run several yards and <u>hit the dirt.</u> Then advance a few more and down again. There is a proper way to fall, but I can't quite get it yet. There are quite a few rocks and I've found several rather unexpectedly.

Our platoon is divided into 4 squads. There is a squad leader for each one and an acting sergeant. I have been sergeant the past week. I call the platoon to attention, dress them up, and report for them to the top sergeant. We take training tests on Saturday afternoon and yesterday our platoon sergeant was giving some of the tests so I took charge all afternoon. What a life the sergeant leads.

I started to tell you about last week and the films. The

We get our rifles...

same day we saw the propaganda film, they took us to a theater for a play. It was pretty good and I enjoyed it a lot.

I turned in my application for Officer Candidate School last Tuesday. It was really a pain to fill out. I never saw so many questions about so many things. If my application is accepted, I'll probably leave here for Ft. Belvoir, Virginia soon after the end of this basic training period (10 more weeks) Sunday before last after I had sealed your letter, I went to supper. There was a boy in our platoon sitting across the table, from Texas. He kept talking to the man on his right like he was from Texas also. I asked him and he was. Then two other boys there at that table said, well so are we! That made 5 of us there, and another surprise! One of them was drafted out of A&M at the same time I was. He was an Engineer at school, from Marlin, Texas, and knew several boys in the band. He said there was another A&M boy here in this Company but I haven't met him yet. He is in some other platoon.

We had a bunch of brass hats here yesterday for inspection. A general inspected the 2nd and 4th platoons. I'm glad he didn't get ours. One of the Lts. said he was going to put a "measles" sign on all the platoons to keep the generals out. The 1st platoon is in quarantine now.

We have all been in two weeks quarantine and got out last night. That means we're not confined to the company area anymore, so as soon as I can, I'll try to see Lt. Schneider.

Everyone here has a horrible cold. Some of the boys nearly have pneumonia. Most of them have bad coughs, but I don't. I really hate to be sick--you miss so much.

I was on K.P. last Tuesday. It is not such hard work, but the hours are long and no breaks for time off. I was lucky, though. They sent for me to go to the hospital in the morning to get my glasses checked. I didn't get back until noon. They are ordering new glasses for me.

We are kept busy all the time. We even have some instruction at night. We have a good platoon sergeant and Lt. We lost one corporal yesterday. He was a swell fellow and we chipped in $10 for him. He's being sent to Cooking school.

I'm going to start drawing pictures and will send them to you. You can get a book to put them in. I'm going to try to get hold of a camera and get some photographs. Never mind the stationery, I'll get what I want at the P.X., now that we're out of quarantine.

I'll try to write again soon. We're pretty well settled so I'll be able to arrange my schedule better.

Lots of love to you all,

James.

Sunday Feb 14, 1943
Ft. Leonard Wood. Mo.

Dearest Family,

I got the package and your letter. I also heard from Mrs. Pratt. Much obliged.

I told you last letter we were going to the range last Monday. I did very well on my firing. I got 70 out of 80 rapid fire for 16 shots and I only got off 15 of my shots. I did fairly well on my slow fire also.

We went on a 11 mile hike Friday afternoon. We went out Wednesday and Thursday into the woods around here and practiced extended order drill, open squad formations, patrols, and capturing machine gun nests, etc. We started out Wednesday morning and ran into an ambush. We hit the dirt at the side of the road and proceeded to surround and extermish them. We combined everything for our hike Friday. We started out with full field pack and our overcoat tied over the top. It really gets heavy, behind me. We were walking along the sides of the road when they hollered "gas!" We whipped on our masks when the sign of "enemy aircraft" came, so we dived into the brush along the sides of the road. Then all clear came and we marched on. Soon we hit a tough hill. They turned loose a smoke bomb and we climbed the hill with our masks on. Puff! Puff! Several men dropped out there.

We marched on after a 10 minute break 'till about 5:30. We started to pitch tents in a wooded area. We had to dig individual slit trenches 2 by 2 by 6 feet. We had two gas attacks there. Every time I put on my glasses, I had to take them off to put my mask on. After chow, we rolled our packs and started out again. The rest of the way was just marching through mud until we hit the road and came on in. We got in about 8:30. Then our Lt. bought candy for the whole platoon and passed it around.

We've also been studying camouflage. That's lots of fun. We practiced putting up flat tops of chicken wire and fish nets. A flat top is a net covered with leaves or strips of cloth to camouflage a machine gun nest, command post, etc.

They also showed us three films on camouflage to be used in the field or at a camp. I really like this part of our training. All of it has been alright so far except for the cold.

We went out last week and had some instruction on road obstacles, Molotov cocktails, and mines. They showed us how to lay mine fields and other things pertinent to mines. We also examined a tank, a half-track, and a reconnaissance car.

You know I told you we were out of quarantine. Well, they told us last week (that) (we) had to (go) back in for a couple of days as we got out too early by several days. Then when we came back from the camouflage area, we found out one of the cooks from our platoon had broken out with the measles. The

whole company is in quarantine and confined to the barracks. Luckily I got to the P.X. for a haircut a day or so before the quarantine. Some of the boys are quite shaggy.

Lots of love to all,

James

Sunday Morning
Ft. Leonard Wood, Mo.

Dear Family,

Another week passed and lots of things covered. They called me in for an interview for O.C.S. last Tuesday. My interviewer was a second lt. who had been through West Texas around Lubbock and south of there. I hope I made a good impression on him. He seemed to think I was a little young, but maybe they won't hold it against me.

They showed us how to set up a gin pole, one of the most used contraptions in Engineers. It consists of a tall pole with 4 guy ropes on it, and is used to raise and move parts of bridges and other heavy objects around a small area.

By slacking up on one rope, you lean the pole the direction you want it.

Most of our work has been on firing this week. We fired two days and fire again today and tomorrow. Record day is Tuesday. I hope my shooting improves by then as I would really like to win a nice medal.

Tuesday
Time does fly, doesn't it? Well, we fired our practice shots last Sunday and I really did swell; 38 out of 40. There are 3 classifications, marksman, sharpshooter, and expert. My luck is the same as usual. We fired for record today and I really shot swell. I had two runs of 16 rounds rapid fire to fire. On the first one I shot 73. I also shot a 70-something on the 300 yard range which is good. I had one run of 16 rounds and needed 71 to qualify as expert, the best. Well, as usual, fate stepped in and what did I do on my last shooting? I shoot a 48. <u>48!</u> So I don't even rate sharp-shooter. I'm just one of the boys who managed to qualify, --just one of the run-of-the-mill jerks, like the ditch-diggers, boiler-makers, and the other low-life. How and why I <u>always</u> have to do something like that, I don't know. I must be cursed or hexed by witches, or something. Coises! Ole Buck Pvt. Mims of the rear rank. I am disgusted. But on to the current history of my life.

Monday we had demolitions. We have learned how fix fuses and fire charges. We each took a small charge of nitro-starch, fixed an electric cap in it, and set it off. We haven't fired dynamite or T.N.T. yet, though.

Tell Uncle Basil best regards and love to you all,
James

Dear Folks,
I think I'm due for guard duty this week-end so I don't guess I'll phone. Maybe I can make it next week. I took my physical exam for O.C.S. I now weigh only 149 and 31 inches around the middle instead of 32. I feel swell. I got your package. Don't send any more candy since I can get it at 3-- per bar.

I'll write soon.

Love,
James

P.S. Also got your letter & Cousin Clari..(letter cuts off)

February 27, 1943
Ft. Wood, Mo.

Dear Folks,
Well, here I sit with a few minutes off--I hope. It's a pretty day out and just what we needed this morning. We were instructed in the use of pioneer earth-moving equipment--i.e. picks and shovels. There's even a G.I. way to use them. We also used air driven saws and hammers and drove a bull-dozer. I really like this out-door life. This isn't the first time we've used to shovels and picks, though. One cold morning we dug fox holes as we did today. This frozen ground is hard to work with and the soil is very rocky.

I told you I had taken my physical exam for O.C.S. I took all my exams and then took the paper to a Lt. to have it O.Rd. He said 20/200 in my right eye was too weak for the Eng. Corps and told me to take my eye test over and see if I would

do better. I went back and memorized the chart while the fellow wasn't looking. I told him what the Lt. said, so he asked me if I could see the second top line at all. I said, "yes", so he said my vision was 20/100 which is a lucky break--I guess! Anyway, I passed my physical.

Thanks a lot for the package of candy. Since I've been in the army, I've had a terrible craving for candy as have the other men here. I guess it's because we burn so much energy. I can buy candy at 3-- a bar and since we're out of quarantine, have no difficulty getting it. I usually carry a bar with me in the morning and evening when we go out.

This week we've studied small arms as anti-aircraft and hand grenades. A grenade isn't thrown like a baseball, but must be lobbed overhead so it will stay where it hits. They are rather heavy. We used dummies with the power taken out. We've also been studying use and care of all carpenter tools.

I'm a little tired now from moving the "pioneer earth", and since it's nearly time for instruction in "pioneer food-moving equipment," the use of which I'm very proficient in, I'll let you go answer the phone, mother, and maybe I can phone you next Sunday afternoon.

Lots of love to all,

James

P.S. I started this letter on my footlocker. That's why you can't read the first part. Don't ask about the second part.

P.S. Was the phone really ringing?

March 17, 1943
Ft. Wood, Mo.

Dear Family,

We traded in our Garands for Springfield's, not that we're through firing. They really got rust on the 25 mile hike we took last Wednesday in the rain. I managed O.K., but my feet really hurt 2 days later.

They called me the other day to see if I wanted in a new E.R.T.C. band they are forming. That would mean stopping my training and no O.C.S. so I didn't consider it. I miss the band work a lot, though.

Last week we used Bangalore torpedoes, long tubes filled with nitro-starch, or other explosive, and used to clear mine fields or barbed wire. They really open a hole in wire. We also made craters(?), used as road blocks. We used 56 sticks of dynamite in our <u>4 line</u> crater. That means the diameter of the holes is 4 times the depth of the hole. It's lots of fun.

We were also introduced to booby traps, little catches which, when released, set off charges of explosive. They are really dangerous to personnel and hard to locate and disarm. They work well in connection with mine fields.

Next week we go to ponton school to make ponton bridges (not pontoon). They don't have any electricity there and you have to shave from canteen cups but they say it's lots of fun.

We're off guard and I'm writing this in the barracks now. I'm beginning to feel a little tired and wish we didn't have to go out tonight.

We have to take combat packs/raincoat & pr. of socks, and gas mask. Each squad will be given a mission to perform with the greatest secrecy possible. A gas attack will probably result if we are discovered.

Lots of love,
James

Sunday 28, 1943

Dear Folks,
Well, I'm back from Ponton school and didn't drown in the river after all! It was really tough work. We were quartered in 6 man huts with a sibley stone and wooden bunks. (G.I. pen) We took our mattress covers and filled them with hay. I never got mine filled so I slept on the boards. It was just about as comfortable. The main inconvenience was no lights. We built everything from light foot bridges to heavy 25 pontons. The difference between a ponton and a pontoon is that a ponton is basically a boat while pontoons are sealed completely. That bridge building is really heavy manual labor. The pontons weigh from 200 to 1800 lbs. For the pneumatic ones the wgt. is about 600 lbs. We double-timed back 60 steps walk and 60 steps run, with full field pack, etc. The sweat just rolled off of me but I made it.

We started our bayonet practice while at ponton school. That is one thing that really turns my stomach, but I hope I can get real good at it.

This next week, we build fixed bridges. We have one night building a bridge under simulated fire. They say that's plenty rough and tough fighting. We have a new corporal who's plenty tough, but as luck would have it, he's from Texas so I have a pretty good suck with him. His home is Dallas. Our platoon commander, Lt. Meggarity is from Beaumont, Texas. I should do all right with them.

They are starting to send some of our increment out already. I may be shipped before long. I haven't heard anything else about O.C.S. as yet.

I can't think of anything else so I guess I'll have to quit.

Lots of love to you all,
James

April 8, 1943

Dear Folks,
They pulled a new one on us Tuesday. We went to the combat range, an open plain crossed by two small streams which we had to cross to attack and drive back an enemy. They located machine guns and a 37 mm anti-tank gun on the hills behind us. We had 20 rounds of live ammunition to fire at card-board targets. We would make a rush of about 5 steps, hit the ground, and listen to the machine gun bullets snap right over our heads. They gave us old type helmets for which I have no use. Every time I hit the ground, it slipped right over my eyes. And it sits right up on the top of your head. I'm still tired and sore from the running around we did out there. We've been making roads this week, included culverts, filling shell holes, building drainage ditches, etc. It's too much work. Tomorrow we build those arched, pre-fabricated barracks.

We only have one more week after this. We have a big parade for the General Saturday, and graduation exercises next week. We also have the worst of all next week, a 53 mile hike. It'll last 2 nights and a day. We build bridges and roads at night and probably won't get more than 5 hours sleep the whole time. Maybe I won't write for a while.

They showed us the iron rations the soldier carries in his field pack. I imagine we'll carry those on the hike.

Can't think of anything else so will go to bed.

Lots of love to all,
James

P.S. I got some films (size B-2, agfa) and will take pictures Sunday if it's sunny.

April 12, 1943
Ft. Leonard Wood, Mo

Dear Folks,
Quite a few of the men here are shipping out this week and they've asked us to ask our correspondents not to write until we send a new address. I'll write again as soon as I can, so don't write until you hear. I may go to the O.C.S. or I may stay here until they need me, I don't know. Then again I may be shipped tomorrow or the next day.

We go on our 50 mile hike tomorrow night so I guess I had better go to bed. You may as well stop the paper till I write again.

Lots of love,
James.

P.S. Use the money for bonds. I kept what I thought I might need if I ship.

Sunday 16, 1943
Ft. Leonard Wood, Mo.

Dearest Family,
I'm still here!

Things were plenty busy last week. The General made an inspection of the 29th Btn. We really had to get things cleaned up. If he inspected more often than six months the

war would have to be stopped so we could get cleaned up.

We put on our khakis yesterday. Today is a beautiful summer day so I finally took some pictures. I have 1 film left and I'll send the role to the William's as soon as I take it.

I was a little surprised at our sudden complete victory in Tunisia, but really glad.

I wish I could come home for awhile. I remember all the good times there and they seem so far away. Gee, it would be nice to sleep in a quiet room and eat one of your good home cooked meals, Mom, and see you all again. Won't it be swell when this mess is through?

Give my regards to all. I haven't time to write.

Lots of love,
James

April 17, 1943
Ft. Leonard Wood, Mo.

Dear Family,
I'm to be here another two weeks to take an O.C.S. refresher course which will give me more detailed training in some of

the work we have covered. Then soon after I guess I will go to O.C.S., unless I don't make the refresher course. Sam Carter will be here another 12 weeks as a corporal, but Gualt is due to be shipped.

We had our final review Sat. and were reviewed by a general. He said our platoon was very good looking and complemented us.

A Lt. Col. inspected the rifles. I came to a snappy "inspection arms" and he said I was a good looking man and didn't look at my rifle, thank goodness!

Our long hike was really rough. We left here Tuesday night, went out a ways and built a road, then came back for our overcoats because it turned off colder. Before we got to our bivouac area, we were all reeling from sleepiness. We dug foxholes and ate breakfast about the time the sun came up. Our company was on the defensive and the other 3 companies were our enemies. Wednesday we captured about 8 of their men and Gualt was the only man we lost. He said that when they questioned him, he talked double-talk and they finally gave up. That night we left the area and hiked to a new one where we dug in to hold against a dawn attack. I was runner for the Capt. and rode in the back of a half-track. Gee! It was really cold back there. Finally a Lt. Col., our Btn C.O., came along in another track and made me get inside the cab where I immediately went to sleep. We had our attack, using blanks and fire-crackers, and then went in to camp. WE had the rest of the day to sleep, which I did.

Love to all,
James

Joplin, Mo.
Sunday

Dear Folks,
The main thing I want to do is go home. You know, I haven't had a home-cooked meal in nearly 5 ½ months. To eat here in town, it costs at least $1.00, and that really adds up. On the bus I got to thinking about home, how I would like to hear Daddy laugh or tickle you, Mother, or Sister. (I got a laugh out of Sister's letter about the "nightgowns".) I was also thinking about the way we used to go to Tyler and how you have laughed, Dad, about that little model A, with the gear hitting my knee and Sister on Mother's lap or up in the back. I laughed right out and everybody on the bus turned and looked at me. Speaking of Tyler, Daddo wrote me a letter the other day. It was nice to hear from him. There is to be a shipment of A.S.J.P. boys to Huntsville, but I don't imagine I can go there. That's too much to hope, when I'll be lucky to go anywhere. Frank Mo. is in Africa, he said.

It is plenty hot now. I'm afraid I'm getting prickly heat again. It is so humid and steamy in this section. I wish I could get back on the dry plains again.

Lots of love and tell Uncle Basil to write when he can,
James

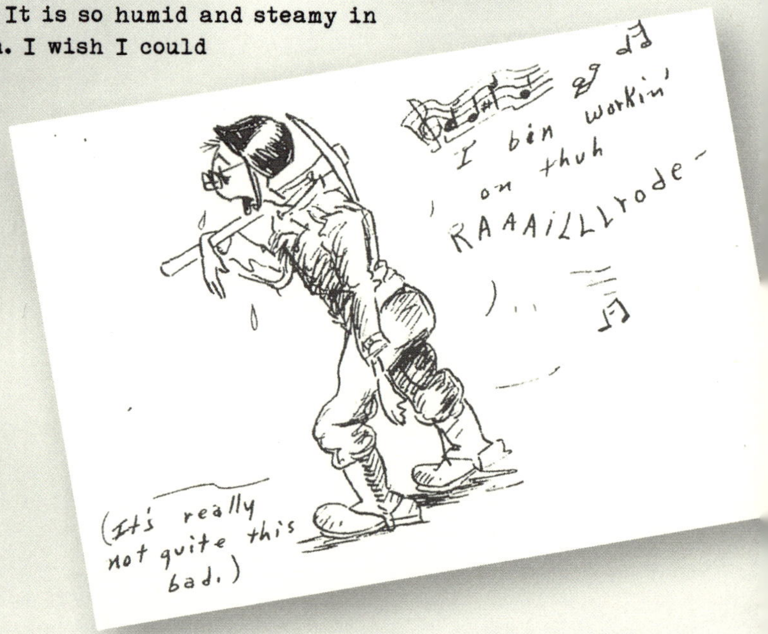

May 20, 1943
Ft. Wood, Mo.

Dear Folks,
My back is bothering me again. Yesterday the O.C.S. board called 70 of the 90 excepted candidates together and told us we couldn't go to school. They handed us our applications book with a note from the General that we were accepted, but had not been sent here and the quota was cut. I can turn it in again in my new outfit, where (word faded) that is.

We will be allowed to apply for A.S.T.P. (Army Specialized Training Program). I did that and was interviewed today, giving languages as my preference. If I'm accepted that will mean several months school which may be a better thing than the O.C.S. anyway.

I went to classification and found I'm due to be here until about the 29th of this month. I tried to get a furlough, but it takes too long to put it through. I applied for a 3 day pass to Jefferson City, though, and should get that. I'll probably send a bunch of stuff home in a few days since I don't know what I'll be allowed to take when I ship. You can send it back if I'm still in the country and need it.

Of course, I was very disappointed, but it couldn't be helped. Anyway, I'm now eligible to be shipped over if I don't go to school.

Nothing else to say now.

Dear Family,
Still here!
Oh yes, the blow finally fell. The 1st sgt. Made me permanent K.P. pusher, dignified by the title, sanitation corporal. I'll have to do that until I leave here. I'm trying to like it because I figure if I can't learn something from everything I do, I'll never be any good at anything. Sgt. Page is going to teach me how to butcher meat. He has some books on it, and he said I could study. I like it a little better but it's from 5:00 'till at least 8:00 every day, Sunday included. I'm getting pretty sleepy.

My dog tags are giving me heat where they rub against me. One day I wear these in front and scratch my stomach and they next day I wear them the other day and scratch my back.

You know, I've really been satisfied with this camp all week; that was because I saw Bataan last Tuesday. After all, I get plenty to eat, clean sheets and a good bed, a roof over my head, candy and ice cream, etc. I could be worse off by a long shot.

The flies are bad here, and you know how I seem to draw them. I have a great ambition. Someday I'm going to kill all the flies in the world! Why, I'd be famous beyond belief.

Love,
James

May 26, 1943
Ft.Wood, Mo.

Dear Folks,

As yet I haven't heard a word about school and nobody seems to know when I'll be notified.

I sent my pants and some stuff for you from Springfield last night. The sun is out today so I'll take my other film and send it and the camera home. I'll try to get a box somewhere for them.

I'm glad Sister got so many nice things for graduation. I knew she would.

I'll write again soon.

Love,

James

Boston College, 1943–1944

My object was to transfer to the Field Artillery and get a commission. That was my branch at A&M and I thought my training there would help me, but I could not manage a transfer. However I had applied for Engineers Officers Candidate School while at Leonard Wood and was one of forty who had been accepted. But quotas were cut and only four actually went. I wasn't one of them. The Army had decided to return a bunch of its soldiers to school and created something new, the Army Specialized Training Program, and we were given the option to enroll in it. I knew enough even at that tender age to jump at the chance, and was accepted to study Spanish. I supposed I would be sent somewhere near home and was shocked when I was assigned to Boston College, in Boston, Massachusetts! This proved, however, to be a wonderful experience. People were very hospitable, we had many varied and interesting experiences, and I got to further my education in safety and comfort while most of those I had trained with were in combat in the South Pacific.

My dorm is building to the left and straight ahead is the Mess Hall on the Grinnell College campus.

July 3, 1944
Grinnell, Iowa

Dear Folks,
Well, I'm not there anymore, or rather, not there. Finally I left on the first on a troop train for here. I got your letters about 2 minutes before I left. It really seemed a little odd to leave the old place. We buzzed up to St. Louis and then on to here. We left the fort about 1:00 P.M. and got here around 6:00 the next morning. You should have seen me trying to sleep on that dratted day coach. I was all cramped and stiff next morning and black from head to foot. These trains are terribly sooty up here & Everything you touch is black. This is beautiful country up here. The ground is black and resembles the gentle rolling laud around Ft. Worth, except it is very green. Of course there is lots of corn neatly planted, but not very high.

This place is only a sort of reception center to determine when we will go to school. This is the first A.S.T.P. bunch in here as this was, up until it was discontinued last month a finance officer candidate school.

This place was founded in 1846, quite an old college. Gary Cooper stayed in the same hall I'm in, but was kicked out of school because his prof told him he'd never be an actor!

We are restricted to the immediate area of the dorms, but even that isn't bad. We were all quite awed by the mess here. After fighting for every bite at Ft. Wood, we came in here, the silver is heavy and very shiney, the food hot, table cloths on the table. We all sat down and didn't know whether to eat or not--and then one of the Lt.'s apologized because the food wasn't up to par!

We nearly collapsed. This is really a beautiful place. The town is small and so is the campus, but it's got a pretty lawn around the dorms which is Old Dutch architecture, three stories high and garret rooms. I would really enjoy going here. There are lots of squirrels around which are very pretty.

I believe I'll have my interview and ship in about 3 days but you can write here if you wish. The address is Co. B.A.S.T. Star Unit, Grinnell

I'm still as anxious to come home as ever, but I'm farther away. It's fairly certain that I'll get at least 5 days home before I'm shipped over.

That is a new law, now Most (2) of my old company are in England now. Three of the boys I slept close to are there. Some went to Alaska, Canada, and the South Pacific. That makes me feel funny.

Mother, do I have any sun tan pants at home from school? I think I have at least one pair that are good. We only have two pair of khakis, so if I have some, send them when I get stationed.

I haven't done much drawing for a long time but I think I'll try to get some soon. I've got more material than I can ever use.

We were told at supper that we could go into town tomorrow from breakfast 'till noon and from 1:00 'till 5:00. That will be very nice.

I'll keep you informed as to how I come out. I think I have a swell chance to get a good course in Spanish at some univ.

Lots of love to all,
James

July 14, 1943
Grinnell, Iowa

Dear Folks,
I'm due to ship out this afternoon at 2:30. I'm going to a place where I can at last come home once in a while--that is, if I could get a 30-day furlough and had about 6 month's pay! I'm going to a place exactly 2120 miles from Midland, Boston College in the suburbs of Boston, Mass. (Bahston!) Why, that's farther north than New York! Do we know anyone there, I doubt?

When I get a furlough, I'll just have to go to N.Y. and stay at the stage door nineteen!

I'll send my address as soon as possible. I got Sister's and Dad's letter.

Love,
James

July 27, 1943
Boston College, Mass

Dear Folks,
I'll just start at Grinnell and bring you up to date:

We left there about midnight and had about 26 of us in a pullman. We were supposed to be 2 in a bottom bunk, but no one was in the uppers so we slept with a blanket up there. It was slow getting to Chicago, which we reached about 10:30 Sunday morning. Sunday afternoon we went on through Indiana and Ohio along by the Great Lakes, I don't know which ones. That country reminds me a lot of bayous of Galveston part of Texas, --flat, salty looking country with seeds etc. Also saw some Cranes. Those lakes are really large, with big tankers, coal ships, and lots of little boats on them. We enjoyed watching in comfort, because we went into the club-car which was air-conditioned. Boy, they had some ritzy cars on that train and we hardly stopped between Chicago and Boston. They had several of these high-powered compartment cars, considerably out of my class. Our coach was rather old, but better than a chain car. There were almost 18 cars on our train.

It was really interesting to watch the scenery and see all the industrialization. It's hard to describe all the factories and chimneys and cranes, etc. Lots of that stuff is right on the lake where the steamers can dock right along side. Quite a different picture from what I'm used to.

We got to Albany or rather Buffalo, N.Y. about midnight Sunday, so I didn't see much of Chicago either, since it was Sunday and I was afraid I'd get lost. It seems pretty large from what I saw of it.

Boston College across reservoir

We got in here to Boston about 10:30 and then came on out to Boston College. This is a Catholic school and I understand the Jesuits will teach some of our classes. I don't specially care for that. This is really a beautiful college, situated on a hill overlooking a small body of water. There are lots of trees and plenty of shrubs. The school is Gothic architecture and beautiful, although I expect it is very expensive.

There are 6 of us in our room on the second floor, all Spanish students. One boy Tom Jones, is from El Paso, knows the Evans, and is a good friend of Bob Grady. We all got a pass into town. We ate some fish and crabs that were very good. Then we went to the U.S.O. and got a swell deal. There are 10 of us going out to Cohassett, about 35 miles from here close to Cape Cod, to some people's estate. There are also 10 French sailors going to be there. We'll spend the whole day there. That will be next Sunday so I'll tell you how we did.

Boston is really 200% nicer than I thought and the people seem swell. We got off of the subway trolley last night coming back to school and a car stopped and gave us a ride. It was a Lt. from Alabama and some young lady from Boston. Tom & I talked to them about an hour and she promised to get us dates. We don't start classes till about August, I believe. There will be about 500 of us here.

One bad thing is the laundry situation. We have to wash our clothes until they can find a place.

We get a weeks leave between semesters and it's only about 350-400 miles to Washington, D.C. Of course, it's close to New York, too. I was hoping I'd get closer to home, but I guess not.

All my love,
James

August 3, 1943

Boston, Mass.

Dearest Family,

Well, true to the Mims luck, I didn't go to Cohassett this past weekend, but lots of other things have happened.

Saturday, Tom Jones from El Paso and I met two British sailors and talked with them for a couple of hours. They took us out and bought us supper. They are on one of those old lend-lease destroyers which was in here at the port. The funniest thing to them about Americans is that "even the <u>Adults</u>" here in this country seem to enjoy "these silly comic strips!" They must have been thinking about Mrs. <u>Prune-face</u>! We all enjoyed it a lot.

Saturday afternoon, we took "a walk on Beacon Hill," where there are the homes of Louisa Mae Alcott, Hawthorne, etc. You would have enjoyed seeing all those old English-type house, just like in a picture show. Some of the streets still have cobble-stones in them. We also saw Paul Revere's grave, John Hancock's, and Mary Goose's--the original Mother Goose. There were lots of old tomb-stones like in Life last week. I haven't been to Bunker Hill yet, but will probably go next Saturday. There are lots of curio shops that are lots of fun to window-shop in. I'm enjoying this a lot, but I can't help but think how much more fun it would be if the whole family were here.

We ride nearly every where on the streetcar which is underground. I'm about to get located with them now. I just ask everybody questions 'till I find out what I want to know.

As I write this I haven't had a letter from you, but I got the wire & money, and the papers forwarded from Grinnell. We haven't been paid because all of the boys aren't here yet. I'll probably get paid in about 10 to 14 days. I really don't need $20.00, but, of course, it helps. Seems as how you need money to get around here.

I'm reading Oliver Wiswell by Kenneth Roberts. The first part is about Boston, and mentions Fremont street and others I've been on. That makes it very interesting.

I'll write again soon.

Love,
James
P.S. I got my promotion to Pfc.--but don't have them put it in the paper--please!

August 3, 1943
Boston, Mass.

Dear Mr. Wemple,
I really have a marvelous chance here in Boston. I'm to study from 3 to 6 months Spanish, along with the History and geography of Latin American countries. It looks like we'll be given a change at a commission to act as Liaison officers. I've now been promoted to Pfc., which is $4.00 extra per month, a the prospect of better ratings to come.

Boston College is a beautiful school, with old Gothic type, stone buildings. We are living in the building which formerly housed the faculty. One boy in our room is from El Paso. His name is J.T. Jones (odd name!) His dad has a Ford business in El Paso. He is also studying Spanish.

Give my regards to the family, please.

Yours truly,
James

August 7, 1943
Chestnut Hill, Mass

Dearest Mother,
Here it is your birthday again! Seems like that happens nearly every year now, doesn't it? Well, many happy returns and here's hoping that I can be home to help you celebrate the next one.

Mother, there are so many things I want to tell you but it just seems like words aren't good enough, or that I don't know the right ones.

First, let me say that you are the best mother any boy ever had or ever will have and I love you just oodles. Gee, how I miss you! It seems that while-you are home, you don't appreciate it nearly enough.

James W. Mims and John Thomas Jones, of El Paso, on roof of Boston College. (Students had access to go up there and study.)

Advanced Spanish class with teachers, señor and señora Eduardo Azuola.

I found that out when I went off to A&M. and have even a greater appreciation from my service in the Army. A fellow meets every kind of person here, and lots of them are not the kind to even be seen with. Maybe I'm being self-centered about it, but so many people haven't had the advantages or the beautiful home that you, Mother and Dad, have given Sister and me. How can I find words to tell you how I appreciate that and thank you for it? Of course you know how I feel--you always know more about me than I know myself. Remember how you could hear my tonsils swelling in the other room.

I remember when I used to be smaller when I would get sick and want everything under the sun--how you would laugh at me. And how much fun I used to have when you would get mad at me--I'd get you tickled. I always love to see you laugh.

Mother, I'm so glad that you and Dad got married. I don't think I'd want to have any other Mom or Dad. And where can I find any other Sister as sweet as mine? You know, I think we've got a pretty swell family, don't you?

I just came back from dinner, and it just added proof that not anyone can cook like you. Gosh, I'd like to have a broiled tongue or lamb roast with some apple pie, etc. It's been seven months to a day that I've been a soldier and I haven't had a home cooked meal all of that time.

Well, I've read this over and it doesn't say what I wanted to, but you know I miss you so much and love you Mother. I do hope that everything I do will make you proud of me because I'm going to try to always do that way.

I'm sending a birthday present for you. Everyone I showed it to, like it and I think you will too. It's the most impractical thing I could find and I hope it surprises you.

I'd like to come home to see you all, but I guess I can't. We are hoping we'll go to South America or Mexico after we finish here, so maybe it won't be too long before I'll see you.

All my love to you, Mother
James

August 14, 1943
Chestnut Hill, Mass.

Dear Mother & Dad,
Well, our first week of school is over and it hasn't been too hard. I'm only taking 2 subjects, but it keeps me busy. I'm going to have to study to keep up as this geography is going to be a little hard to remember.

I have a fine Spanish teacher here. Her name is Mrs. Azuola or Senora de Azuola. Her husband is the consul for Costa Rica, but both of them teach out here. We have lots of fun in class. Her English is not too good and we like to tease her about her pronunciation. I've gotten to where I can understand Spanish fairly well, but I can't speak too well as yet.

Love to you both,
James

August 21, 1943
Boston, Mass.

Dear Sis,
I'm supposed to be changed to the advanced Spanish class Monday. I was supposed to be in it from the first, but wound up in medium. Boy, this geog. is tough. We have a quiz each Sat. morning and they are really tough! I think I flunked it, but I hope not. The questions are very badly worded and you really have to know everything about the subject to answer them.

Say, what course do you plan to study at T.S.C.W.? Are you going to take any Spanish?

Well, I'm going into town for the afternoon, so I'll quit. Give my regards to the Williams' family.

Love,
James

August 28, 1943
Boston, Mass

Dear Family,
My studies are coming along pretty good, but we really keep busy. We had a rather difficult geography lesson last week with a couple of intricate maps. Reminds me of the 6th grade. Also had to read a Spanish novel and have yet to write my report on it. Both Senor and Senora Azuola are very well educated and most interesting. Last week I gave a Spanish talk on my home town. I really painted a swell picture of the whole thing.

We've moved again to room 216. Tom and I are together with a James McLachlan from Detroit. We have a pretty nice room, but I hated to break up our other bunch which was very nice.

I made an 80 & an 85 on my first 2 geography quizzes and the one Sat. seemed fairly easy. We are due for a monthly quiz next week. It may be harder.

Love to you all,
James

September 21, 1943
Boston College

Dear Folks,
We have entered a new phase of our work. After the first six weeks of general European geography we are receiving the next 6 weeks in Spanish geography. I think I told you our geo. prof. wasn't so hot, and we got him again. Senor de Azuola says "if he says anything wrong about my wife's home, I will publicly deny him in my classes, even if it costs me my zhob!" He's really a swell prof. and funny as the dickens.

We laughed 'till we couldn't see. Maybe he was having just as much fun, who knows.

You asked me, mother, if we still have a third boy in the room. Yes, he's still with us (letter cuts off) from Detroit.

This A.S.T.P. looks better all the time The (cut off) is a rumor which seems to be a bit stronger than some that a few of the graduates from this receive their commission on getting out. Sounds good, anyway. They have designed a shoulder patch which is supposed to be out by November.

James W. Mims on roof at Boston College.

Then, too often we finish our course, we will receive a certificate which states that so-and-so has complete the Army of U.S. training course in A.S.T.P. and that the grades are on file. These certificates are then to be used to obtain credit, in my case, at A&M if they will accept the course. Certainly, I should get credit for the Spanish when I go back.

Postcard of Washington D.C.

You said you're glad that I get to see somewhere besides Texas, but the only thing it's done is to make me sure I don't want to live anywhere but Texas. This part of the world just isn't human compared to Texas. Did you know I've been away for nearly 9 months now? Seems short yet an awfully long time.

Do you think I should try to come home for my week's furlough or not? Naturally, I would like to come, but it is so far I don't believe I could make it. Tom and I are going out to the airport here to see if there is anything at all like a schedule for planes being ferried in that direction by the army. I don't think we'll have any luck with that though, and it will cost too much to go by train and take too long, anyway. I think I'd better plan on going to Washington to see Cousin Percy. That will be lots of fun, but of course, not like coming home.

I can't think of anything else to write. Of course I'll remember something when I seal the letter!

Love to all,
James

October 5, 1943

Dear Folks,
There is a guy here from Ft. Leonard Wood who was in the same refresher course for O.C.S. that I was. He told me that Saturday he saw another one of our bunch who had gone to Belvoir and had received his commission. Just think! I should have gotten mine by now, too. I don't know whether I'm better off or not, but there's still hope of a commission from here.

Tom has written his cousin, Marvin Jones, in Washington and plans on going there if things work out. I guess Cousin Percy & Margaret could put us both up, but I hate to ask them. The other way will work out O.K. The furlough starts about the 31st.

There doesn't seem to be anything else to say so I may as well stop. Write whenever you can and tell me what everyone is doing. I got the high school news and it really seems strange to think of those little squirts playing on the football team, etc!

Tell the folks at the office "hello" for me and write again soon,

Love to you, Mother and Daddy--
James

October 11, 1943

Dear Mother and Dad,
The govt. has a nice present for me. They have cooked up a comprehensive exam for the 18th, 19th & 20th to see how much we've learned. We got our 2 month's grade Saturday & surprise! I cracked 90 on both of my subjects: 90 in geography and 91 in Spanish. How they could add my geography grades and get that score is beyond me, but I'm not complaining of course.

Maybe before long there will be a clarification of our ultimate aims in A.S.T.P. At a meeting of A.S.T.P. officials & representatives of the colleges in St. Louis, a petition was sent that the war department give some indication of what we will receive in the way of a rating when we finish here.

Can't think of another thing to write. If you all have time, come up to see me sometime and I'll show you Boston. Give everyone my regards.

Love,
James

October 20, 1943

Dear Mother and Dad,
I had thought to wait 'till the packages came, but they are a little slow, so I'm writing anyway. I'll write you again when they come, which should be tomorrow.

A fellow named Carl Reavis sent me a letter today. He is one of the men with whom I trained last January in Leonard Wood. I had written him last July when I was in Grinnell, but he didn't get the letter till the 7th of this month since he is on some island, he couldn't say which in the S. Pacific. He said that there are about 4 other fellows still with him who were in my platoon and that they have already seen combat service--he didn't mention what kind or what it was like. That really made me feel funny. Gee, but I'm lucky to have the break I have. I'm hoping I'll be assigned to Intelligence Corps after here, and not to engineers or other combat branch, though we still have no idea at all.

We signed on furloughs today. I'm going to write Cousin Percy & Margaret this week what time to expect me. We get off Sat. the 30th. What did I say in my last letter about a furlough? You said something about thinking it wasn't till the end of this month, which is right! What would you suggest I take along to eat? Please let me know before next week so I can get it then.

Tell everyone I think about them even if I don't write! Tell your son "Basil" my love to him, too.

Love to you all,
James

November 1, 1943
Washington, D.C.

Dear Family,
Well, here I am in Washington in one piece. We came on down on the train yesterday, which took about 9 hours. The folks met me at the station and Tom came on out & slept here last night. He went on out to see Marvin Jones and are planning to stay with him. Cousin Percy got us both passes good for this week at the field and Tom may come back out here to stay. We don't know yet. Of course the children are both swell and lots of fun and Cousin Margaret & Percy enjoy them a lot. They have a very nice house with lots of room and are both rather well satisfied. We, Tom and I, will start sightseeing tomorrow. I'll bet we have a swell time.

We got our furloughs Sunday morning, left at 9:00, and came thru Rhode Island, New York City, Baltimore, Philadelphia, New Haven, Newark ("Newick") and lots of other places I've always heard about. We saw the "Life Saver Factory," the "Singer Sewing Machine Factory", and lots of others. This country is a mess though. There are acres of dirty apartment houses, exactly alike, and jammed all together. I'll write more later.

Love,
James

November 24, 1943

Dearest Mother & Dad,
Your letters came in and I dropped a note to Bob at Devens telling him where to get in touch with me. The paper for wrapping the gifts and Tom's gift came. I don't know if I can wait till his birthday to give it to him or not as I am very curious.

I sent the pictures we took in Washington to Sister and she will send them on to you. They turned out real well, it seemed to me. I've had some good luck with that little box camera.

We got a comforter today. It has been right cool, but they must be expecting colder weather. I am.

I love you all very much,
James

December 8, 1943

Dear Mother & Dad,
I'm C. Q. (Charge of Quarters) tonight so I'm finally getting around to writing. It was very nice to talk to you last Sunday, Mother, and I'm sorry I didn't get to talk to you, Dad. Guess you've got some new roads all lined up.

Sunday afternoon we went to the Artayetas house. They are the consul and his wife from Argentina and she is a Mrs. Wyatt in Spanish. I heard so much of that stuff that I was groggy! We met Mr. & Mrs. Artayeta, one Erick Krac who is studying chem. at M.I.T. and a doctor whose name I've forgotten, all Argentine. We eat supper here at 4:00 Sunday, so we were late. Señora Artayeta insisted that we have something with her, so she fixed soup and coffee & gave us a sandwich of goose. She wouldn't think of our leaving. So we told her that now she was our "Mother" and she liked that very much. She is really full of energy. The señor looks exactly like a man with tweeds, monocle, & all. He is quite a character.

They remind me a lot of Texas people.

Because of former experience, I was one of several guys who give instruction in drill, now. Such things as drilling, facings, and marching. Reminds me of old days in Leonard Wood.

I'm very tired of school. IT's very much like A&M yet we seem to never to have any time. It's a long day from 6:30 'till 11:00 and it's really hard to get out of those warm beds these cold mornings. No snow as yet, though it won't be long 'till we really get it.

Can't think of anything else right now. I believe I'll try to come home on my next furlough. Could you meet me some where or should I come all the way home? Tell me what you think the next time you write & did you send the recipe for the prailines?

All my love,
James

February 13, 1944
Fort Devens, Mass

Dear Mother and Dad,
Here's what has happened, but don't tell this to anyone as it's more or less secret. We came up here last Tuesday for 2 days to get a physical, bringing only our packs, cartridge belts, etc. We didn't do a thing for a couple of days, then went back to B.C. long enough to get all our G.I. equipment. We went over an infiltration course, crawling under barb wire with machine gun bullets whizzing over, had a lecture in malaria, and that's about all we've done. We get our physical exam tomorrow. It snowed and has been plenty cold, reminding me of Leonard Wood, - all this after congratulating myself on not having to be out in it this winter. We also got new dog tags, a film on mail censorship, and filled out the enclosed business for power of attorney. That's so Dad can handle my vast estates and ranches and oil wells! I'm positive we're on our way overseas. Here's what happened about that furlough I wrote about.

As I said, we were only supposed to be in Devens 2 days, then report to our new post on the 24th. The Lt. at school promised us a delay in route so that we'd have time for a trip home before the (CUT OFF) only chance to come home will be if I can get a furlough from where ever I'm sent. I have no idea of my disposition, nor have any of us. The most of the group are French & German with three or 4 Spanish students. This is the result of the exam I told you about, and no one seems to know anything. Continue to write me at Boston, and if there is something extra-special, you could phone Tom. I think he's lost since I left. I wish he could have come with me.

When we do get through here, we'll go back to Boston College and then ship out from there. Looks like I'll see Europe, yet.

We were to make wills if we wanted to, but it's not necessary, I believe.

I'll write again soon,
James

The other letter is for public consumption--this one is <u>not</u>. Tomorrow I go to Ft. Devons for a physical and will be there a couple of days. If I pass that, as I'm pretty sure I will, I come back here before going to my <u>new</u> post, and I think I will receive a "<u>delay in route</u>" --enough to come home on. I don't know the nature of the new assignment, but only 2 of us in the Spanish group are in the small group. Tom is not going. <u>Don't Say Anything About This</u>, but if I should be home about Monday or Tuesday, don't be surprised. My fingers are crossed, but who knows. This is what I told you about, Dad, and whether it means overseas or not, I don't know. Just keep writing me here if you don't get a letter from me for a while, but I'm <u>fairly</u> sure I'll be able to be home for a few days by the time you get this.

Love,
James

Camp Ritchie, 1944

Then one day in February 1944, a team of officers and enlisted men came to the campus and interviewed a number of us, choosing twenty-six for a special assignment. We went to Fort Devens processing and could not figure out what was afoot. We soon learned that we were going to Camp Ritchie, Maryland—the Military Intelligence Training Center! We were told not to tell anybody anything, and that we would be checked back home by the FBI! A new and most interesting world was about to open.

Ritchie was in a beautiful location in the Catoctin Mountains of western Maryland. There was a lake in the middle, it had permanent brick barracks, and was not very large. We were to study Combat Intelligence. Under this heading were several different courses. There was German Interrogator Prisoner of War (IPW); Order of Battle (OB), which is the science of keeping track of enemy units and even individual personnel; MIS, which trained French speaking teams who would work with and reestablish local governments when we got back into France; some Counter Intelligence (CIC); and Photo Interpretation (PI), the study of aerial photos for all kinds of information, and I was assigned to this. We were also trained in reconnaissance patrolling. Our work week was seven days long with every eighth day a holiday, called "Ban Day" after General Banfill, the commandant.

The educational level of men and officers in the camp was exceptionally high. One entry requirement was fluency in at least one other language. Many spoke five or more! There were many German and Austrian refugees, mostly Jewish, and it was not unusual when you asked someone where they were from to be told in a very thick accent, "Hamburg," or some other foreign city! For some reason few of them had had basic training and therefore had no soldier skills. We felt that they were selfish and goldbricks and generally found them not compatible. Because of their background, they were all IPWs, or "I Piddle Diddles," as we called them.

Our training was rigorous with lots of field problems. On one outdoor mapping exercise, the water froze in my canteen! One training problem divided us into small patrols of ten men each, dropped us off after dark out in the mountains with nothing but a French or German map of the area and our compass, told us to meet at a certain place at a certain time, and to avoid the enemy patrols, GIs dressed in German uniforms! We were supposed to orient ourselves, set a compass course, hike through the woods to our destination, and not get caught by the "Germans"! Fortunately there were always little farm boys on bicycles who for a dollar or so would help out by telling us where we were! It was realistic training and sobering to think about doing it in combat. We referred to this activity as "snooping and pooping"!

Since we were only about seventy miles from Washington, D.C. we were always having visitors of all kinds. We saw uniforms we could not begin to recognize! We just saluted them all! But we did have to learn to identify the uniforms and all the insignia of the Germans, Italians, and Japs, their weapons, mechanical equipment, how their armies were organized, and countless other things. We studied captured German, Italian, and Jap equipment. One exercise involved manning an observation post up on the side of a mountain overlooking the Cumberland Valley while various pieces of German equipment maneuvered below. The task was to identify the kind of unit from what we had seen and report it by field telephone to "HQ." Unfortunately this took place in the spring and sitting in the sun after a long cold winter wasn't conducive to staying awake.

One three-day problem simulated the combat intelligence function for units from the Battalion level up to the Corps. About twenty teams were scattered out in the woods and mountains, each representing one of the units. We operated as patrols, had to locate each unit by map, and then hike to it using compass headings, work some specific problem while there, then move on to the next, always avoiding the "Germans." We ate field rations, slept in the pup tents, and got a taste of how it would be in combat. One fellow got cited for a successful counter intelligence action. He got in one tent, found the code book, and burned it without being caught! Unfortunately he also found some poison ivy which he got all over his arms and hands, so General Banfill declined to shake hands with him at the critique ceremony. He just saluted instead.

We were working one photo interpretation problem studying the coast of France mapping the various defenses. Imagine our surprise and delight when we discovered that the Invasion of D-Day was taking place at this site and at the very time we were studying it! We had the combat films from the invasion at the end of that week before any of them were released to the public. From my study of the area I don't see how anyone landed there and lived. The defenses looked impregnable.

We worked with stereo pairs of photos. Using a stereoscope to get three dimension, we looked for all kinds of fortifications, enemy storage depots, anything that would make good artillery targets, and other things. We could measure the exact length of bridges or width of rivers for the engineers, or find good forward observation posts for the artillery. We could either plot all this on a map, or make our own maps when we had poor ones, as on Leyte and Mindanao. It was truly a useful and necessary skill.

March 5, 1944
Camp Ritchie, Maryland

Dear Mother & Dad,
You must think I've been discontinued! As things look now, I'll be here in Camp Ritchie for probably a couple of months for some specialized training, the nature of which I cannot disclose. It is essential that no one know of this. Just say I'm getting "further training" before going overseas. I believe school started about the 10th and we go a 7 day week with the 8th day off.

It has been bitterly cold several days this week with 2 snows. Many of the men here are A.S.T.P. men, some formerly in the air corps, who have not had much basic. Because of that there has been established a refresher course which includes short hikes, manual of arms, firing on the rifle range and other such courses in the school of the soldier. A few changes have been made since I left basic, but most all is old stuff. Just re-read the letters I wrote from Leonard Wood and you'll get an idea. The past week we had some 56 hours work so you can see how busy I've been. We spent one night (Friday) in pup-tents. It was the nicest night this week but still too cold to sleep on the ground. I also had a yellow-fever and typhus shot, which gave us all a little fever. Though the hikes (2) were very short and easy, 6 months as a "U.S.O. commando" has left me in a rather soft condition and tired me, exerting unused muscles. One morning was terribly cold, with a strong wind which gave us all a nice wind-burn.

We have a good chance of O.C.S. after our course, but at present only infantry is open. Should we receive a commission there, I think we would still remain in our present work. I'll make inquiries. We are expecting good ratings when we are placed on completion of our course--as high as master sergeants. That sounds good to me, so I may not be interested in O.C.S.

Unless there is anything special, I won't make an extra effort to phone. There is not much I could tell you, but if you want me to, write and I'll wire when to expect a call. When classes start, we have free time from 5:00 'till the next morning. We get class B passes, which allow us off the post, but there is nowhere to go except the U.S.O., which is right outside the camp. Baltimore is about 80 miles from here and it's not far to Washington. I wrote Cousin Margaret & Percy where I was and that I might have a chance to see them soon. Haven't had an answer yet.

I seem to have run out of material, so I'll close up shop for a while. My regards to everyone.

Love,
James

March 12, 1944

Dear Mother and Dad,
This is awful. I can't write and tell you everything that's happened, but it's all very interesting. Have to wait 'till after the war. But as far as everyone is concerned, it's necessary that they just continue to think that this is "advanced specialized training" before going overseas. That is all that anyone must know. <u>This is imperative</u>! That's all I'll write about that, but anything you find out about what I'm doing must be a secret.

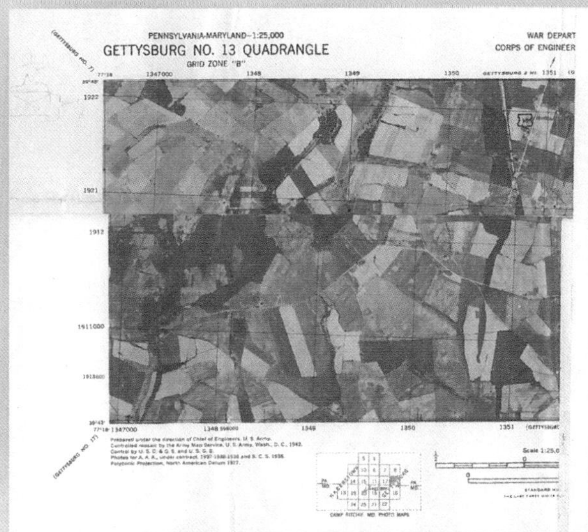

Aerial photo of Gettysburg, Pennsylvania

We started our school yesterday and I'm really pooped already! We go from 7:00 'till 11:30 and from 12:15 'till about 5:00 with night problems frequently. This is for 7 days. Seems funny to study Sat. night and go to school Sunday, but I guess we'll get used to it. Jerry, Schles, and I are in different sections, but we still run around together. Our 8th day is free and called "ban day." That comes Tuesday but I'm not going anywhere except maybe Haggerstown. We're close to the Gettysburg battlefield here, so maybe I'll see that one of these 7 days!

Love to all,
James

12 May, 1944

Dear Folks,
Thanks for the letter. I enjoyed it a lot. They break up the monotony of something different every minute!

We graduated and are now "specialists." There are so many of Hitler's children here who have terrific accents and think that America owes them a living. They figure being specialists, they shouldn't do a thing. The graduation was quite impressive. General Bissell came up and shook us all by hand personally. I got a beautiful diploma with all kinds of signatures on it. I'll bring it home some day soon.

Here's the present set-up. We have about 10 days school. After that, furloughs start for those who haven't had one in 6 months. We'll probably be alerted then and get our stripes and furloughs. At that rate, it looks like June will be my furlough date. How much notice would you need if I came home? Quite a few boys have been suddenly alerted and furloughed immediately so, as usual, I don't know. Expect me when you see me.

It's time for lights out so I'll close.

Love,
James

14 June, 1944

Dear Folks,
I just sent a box of junk home and insured it for $15.00. My watch is in it somewhere, and a bunch of other stuff I either can't use or want to keep. There's nothing in it which you can't open, as I got rid of all that. I still have my grip and a pair of pants which I'll send this afternoon or tomorrow. We really don't know when we leave, but it will be soon, I guess. I bought another address book and am sending the old one home so I'll have a copy of some addresses I don't want to lose.

Receives Promotion

James W. Mims, son of Mr. and Mrs. Percy Mims, 210 East Tennessee, has been promoted from private first class to staff sergeant. Sergeant Mims is stationed at Camp Ritchie, Md.

June 6 1944

My promotion came through last Tuesday. I made a new allotment of $40.00 cash which should start coming in a month or so. If I don't need the money I get, I'll increase that or start buying a $50.00 bond a month. That will depend on our location, of course. I'll have to get busy and sew on my stripes. Three up and a "rocker," which makes me a "1st 3 grader." I'm second on our team and have the exact rating I want. We have a good team and the one officer who goes with us, that I've met, is very good. Don't know the other one yet.

Love,
James

June 17, 1944

Dear Folks,
Boy, is it hot today! I'm burning up.

By the time you get this the box should be there. Bet you couldn't even put anything else in there, Mother! I put in a dry can of "C" ration which you might like to sample.

Thought you would be interested, Dad. See how you like the "coffee." The cocoa is very good, so you can fix that some night for a pepper-upper! Schles went home for 3 days last night and he's going to send my traveling bag and an address book. I copied the ones I needed, but if I should lose it, I'll have that one at home.

Uncle Basil wrote the other day and I enjoyed his letter. There may not be much doing in Midland, but I'd like to help what ever is going on.

There just isn't anything special happening. The under-secretary of war was here the other day and some big-wigs are on the post today, but they are so busy I just don't get to talk with them much!

Lots of love and I'll write as often as I can to keep you in touch.

James

June 20, 1944

Dear Folks,
This is just to let you know of a slight change in address. I've been informed my mail will best reach me at A.P.O. № 5467, c/o Postmaster San Francisco. I do get around, don't I? We'll see lots of interesting country before I get home again, won't I. The only trouble is, we don't have time to stop and see the sights.

Pass my new address around, will you, and I'll write as soon as possible.
All my love,
James

Somewhere in U.S.
24 June, 1944

Dear Folks,
As usual, I can't think of anything to write that's interesting, and yet won't be cut out. Anyhow, I've certainly seen the country, some of our most beautiful, too. I think that after the war I'm going to buy a jeep or a horse and just travel all over the states, climb the mountains, investigate the cave, and see everything.

We stopped for a few hours in St. Louis and had a good bath in the Y.M.C.A. and also in Ogden, Utah, where we went to the guy in the Weber College. The fellow turned on the steam room for us, and then we had a cold shower. That was really a pepper-upper after the sooty train. Ogden is certainly in a beautiful location with tremendous snow-capped peaks in the background.

We had a few hours in Grand Junction, Colorado. After the war, we'll all have to come to Colorado. Gee, but it's beautiful with those mountains--and it's high and cool, with lots of rivers. Both the Arkansas and the Eagle river in the same tunnel, but go in different directions to drain into the Mississippi and the Colorado rivers. I liked Kansas, too, with great plains of wheat. It looked a lot like home and I saw several jack-rabbits. We passed through a big prairie dog town, the dogs fat as pigs and bold as brass. Lots of these boys from the East were quite interested and there were lots of things I could tell them--even as to what a cattle-guard is.

At present, I can't tell you just where I am, but I'm hoping for a pass to investigate some of the nearby cities. This camp is located in a most desolate place, and looks like the place George did his sweeping job! That still gives me a big laugh--it's so typical of some of the things the army does. They gave us ______, probably the last toxin known to man, because I can't think of anything but _______ that we haven't been given ______ for. Cousin Percy said at Bolling they even have one for laziness! It's just a shot of rubbing alcohol & after the first shot, the mere threat of the needle does the trick. They gave that to one boy and Cousin Percy said he did fine after that!

Love to all,
James

2 July, 1944

Dear Folks,
It's very hard to write letters and not break censorship rules, but perhaps this will do.

We have a mascot in the barracks, a cat, with 2 new born kittens. They don't even have their eyes open yet! There were 3 but one of them died day before yesterday. As you know, I'm somewhat of an authority on kittens, but will probably let their mother take care of them, since I have no eye dropper! We're trying to figure a way to take them along with us, but don't quite know how that will go. It's probably against regulations, anyway.

We've been getting various types of training, such as the obstacle course and hikes with packs, -just like basic. The climate here is very similar to Midland's, which means a good hot sun. You can get cool in the shade, but as a rule, you collapse before you can find any! The nights are nice, though, and I'm getting a good tan playing volleyball and just being outside. Food isn't bad, but is heavy for such heat. As usual, I'm always hungry. The P.X. makes very good, thick milkshakes or malts and I can easily keep out of condition.

The Military Intelligence Training Center
UNITED STATES ARMY
CAMP RITCHIE MARYLAND
This is to certify that
James W. Mims 38438243 Pfc
has satisfactorily completed the course prescribed for
the 17th class at
THE MILITARY INTELLIGENCE TRAINING CENTER
Assistant Commandant
Commandant
Director of Training
8 May 1944
Camp Ritchie, Md.
6850

Certificate of Completion, Camp Ritchie

Last week we saw the sixth of 7 films about the war put out by the War Dept. Of course, they are propaganda films, but very good nevertheless. This one is on China and contained pictures captured from the Japs and some made by missionaries during the rape of Nanking. You just can't imagine the horrors committed by these Sons of "Heaven." People with arms that bend between the joints! One fellow had a chunk a couple of inches thick taken out of the back of his neck, and of course the usual treatment of all women. It's horrible to imagine, much less see. It fitted in very well with the March of Time we saw last night on India, showing our overall strategy in that area. We saw cargo planes "flying the hump" from India to China--probably the route Tommy Wilson flies. You'd really enjoy these pictures, Daddy, for they give a pretty good resumé of what's going on.

All my love,
James

New Guinea, 1944

Our group, composed of 23 Photo Interpretation Teams, left Camp Ritchie on our own troop train about June 20, 1944. Each team had either a 1st Lt. or Captain as Officer in Charge, a 2nd Lt., a M/Sgt., a S/Sgt, and two T/3's., lots of brass and rank. A baggage car was set up as a kitchen and all the enlisted men drew KP. Our destination was Camp Stoneman, near Richmond, California, the Point of Embarkation. The trip was quite an experience, but uneventful . . . except for losing M/Sgt. Bryant in Grand Junction! Bryant was an artist and an eight ball! He had already discovered that he had left his dog tags at Richie, a serious mistake. He had gone swimming in the lake in the middle of the Camp the day we shipped out. He had taken off his dog tags, placed them and his billfold under a rock, and left them! Imagine the problem of trying to send a telegram to the MPs telling them how to find the correct rock! (Happily, they did.) When we stopped to change engines in Grand Junction, Bryant climbed up on the tender to make a sketch of the engine crew. He was totally unaware when the engine was uncoupled and taken to the roundhouse with him still aboard. Finally he was retrieved and we went on our way.

At Camp Stoneman, we moved into our barracks, but Bryant couldn't unlock his barracks bag, since his key was on his missing dog tag chain, so he went off to the supply room to get a hack saw. In his absences, we discovered we had a key that would fit, and opened the lock and the bag. Bryant was gone a long time. When he finally returned, he had with him the Supply Sergeant. Because Supply Sergeants are personally responsible for all equipment assigned to them, he was certainly not going to surrender a saw or anything else to someone getting ready to leave the country. Bryant was of course surprised to find his bag open, and nobody offered any explanation. The Supply Sergeant glared at Bryant, muttered some appropriate descriptive words, and stomped out. Shortly Bryant went out, and of course strangely his bag got locked up again! When he returned he was quite puzzled, but no one seemed to know anything about it. So, off his went again to the Supply Sergeant. This time he came back with the hacksaw . . . finally. And of course the bag was open again. Only then did it dawn on him what was going on.

It was hot and dry at Stoneman, and the rolling landscape was covered with dead brownish grass with little brush. I got a weekend pass into San Francisco and together with Stan Mallory and Hugh Luiggi hitch-hiked in. We were in khakis and burning up, and couldn't figure out why soldiers going the other way were in ODs, but we found out that night. Once you drop over the divide and down into Frisco, it gets cold and very uncomfortable when the sun goes down. But we had a good time sightseeing in the short time we had.

And then came the big day when they loaded us up on boats, took us down the river, and we boarded the USS *Seasnipe* late in the afternoon. We assumed we would lay around the harbor for hours . . . waiting. But not this time! By dusk we were sailing under the Golden Gate Bridge to join our convoy. But, surprise! There was no convoy, just our ship! We felt very lonely, apprehensive, and forlorn. Plus lots of fellows were seasick. Fortunately I was not one of them.

The USS *Seasnipe* was my first experience on the ocean. And a troop ship is not a luxury liner by any means. Crowded, hot and stuffy, everyone bored and apprehensive, time hangs heavy. Stan Mallory and I got an assignment working in the Chaplain's office, which was a real stroke of good luck. I became Master of Ceremonies of the nightly amateur shows, and Stan put together an orchestra. The office was about 7 feet wide and about 10 feet long, contained a library, and games, cards, etc., which we would check out to the troops. It was scarcely more than a large closet with a dutch door.

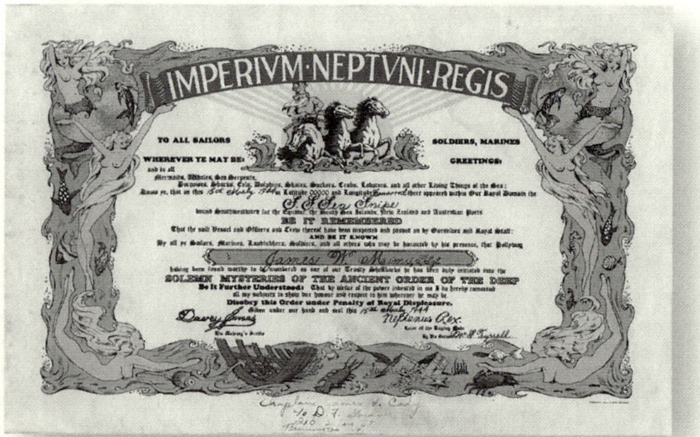
IMPERIVM·NEPTVNI·REGIS

TO ALL SAILORS WHEREVER YE MAY BE: SOLDIERS, MARINES GREETINGS:

BE IT REMEMBERED

SOLEMN MYSTERIES OF THE ANCIENT ORDER OF THE DEEP

Certificate for crossing the Equator

We slept in the office because it had a small fan. One of us would sleep on the desk with feet hanging over, and the other on the floor partly under the desk. We had one storm which I thought was pretty rough. I wedged myself up on the desk and in the corner and read through most of it. We also had one sub scare. But generally the weather was balmy, we could watch the flying fish, and listen to the swish as the ship sailed through the water, or at night, watch the phosphorescent wake from the stern.

I met a fellow from Texas named Maas, who was one of the large number of replacements on board. He used to tease me about my watch with the luminous dial, saying "Sarge, the Japs are gonna see that and torpedo us!" I saw him again at Dobadura, and still later at Hollandia when he was assigned to the combat MPs with our Division.

We had a big time when we crossed the equator. We had all kinds of foolishness and stunts for our initiation, and everyone received a certificate showing "Maly" instead of "July," which was to fool the Japs in case we got captured. All lettering on the certificate done by . . . Sgt. Bryant!

Our first landfall was Milne Bay, New Guinea. My first impression was how incredibly green everything was. The land rose right up out of the water and was covered in jungle. We could see native huts on stilts along the shore, native boats, and all kinds of ships and boats scurrying around. Deeper into the bay we could see all the installations. We were there about two weeks while they unloaded a lot of the ammunition and other supplies we carried. I will never forget one of the dockworkers, a blond fellow, who had let his beard grow long. He worked without a shirt, and was tanned a deep mahogany. The color combination was striking.

We soon moved on up the coast to Oro Bay. We came down the gangplank onto a floating dock out in the bay, then by Dukw to shore, then inland twenty miles to Dobadura, where the Fifth Replacement Depot was. This was to be our home for the next several weeks. (Bryant was the last one down the ladder. He had been drawing!)

We had a very comfortable set up in Dobadura. We made log frameworks on top of which we erected our squad tents, extending out the sides like awnings. We made frameworks over our cots to hold our mosquito bars, or nets, and put our clothes on top. We took beer cans, filled them with diesel oil, cut a piece of tent rope as a wick, and made lamps. They were very smoky, but did give some light. Mallory and I had gotten a copy of the Book of Hoyle from the ship, and we played our way through it.

A major project concerned everyone, and that was constructing showers. There were many ingenious contraptions invented for providing one of our most important needs, the bath!

We were lectured by an Australian officer who had come over the Sananada Trail through the Owen Stanley Mountains, which was quite an achievement. He had been in mining in New Guinea before the war, and told us lots of things about the country, the people, and the culture. The Aussies really had a hatred for the Japs.

All our equipment came and we went to work putting it together. Each team had a Jeep, a small trailer, and a truck. These were in wooden crates and had to be uncrated, the wheels put on, and then tested. Lt. Miller had us build side boards on our trailer. And we had a bunch of other gear, such as a small kit for developing and printing photos. It was very hot work in the tropical sun. I was on top of a crate using an ax to cut the steel bands that held it together. I put the ax down, jumped off, and reached for the ax. The exposed jagged edge of one of the bands cut my arm, which got me taken to the doctor for some stitches, and back to the tent out of the sun for a while. A poor way to get out of work.

The 11th Airborne Division was stationed at Dobadura. We would see the planes as they circled the area and practiced air drops almost daily. The terrain was generally flat and covered with kunai grass which grew 6 to 7 feet tall. There were cobras and boa constrictors, great rats, and who knows what else inhabiting these drop areas, and stories abounded about unfavorable encounters. It was also said that every member of the division had his own jeep, and they were referred to as Ali Babba and his 40,000 thieves!

So, we established a motor pool and had 24-hour armed guards. One moonlit night Packard, Baras, and I were on duty, and we saw something running down the middle of the area. It turned out to be a wallaby bounding along, probably as startled as we.

Maas, the Texan I had met on shipboard, was on nightguard at a bridge at the entrance to our area, and had a real fright. They had heard noises in the adjacent jungle for several nights, and then one night a truck was coming into the area and they stopped it for identification, when they saw in the headlights a great snake across the road! The truck ran over it with the front wheels, and it coiled around the hood. They could not kill it with a carbine, but finally did with a Thompson sub machine gun. That was what had caused all the noise. It was a very spooky place!

Business began to pick up for us the end of the first week of October. We got our orders to report to the 24th Infantry Division, and Lt. Miller, M/Sgt. Packard and I were flown up to Hollandia to join them, leaving the other three men and all the equipment to follow. Weather caused us to have to land at Lae on an airfield cut out of the jungle. We came in over the ocean and seemed to almost run into the trees before we stopped. Then we were taken inland to Nadzab, a big airfield, to wait for further transportation. There I ran into Lt. Jim Inglehart, one of my A&M seniors, a flier, on his way to Australia for furlough. Jim was later killed in combat. He told me we better get on up to Hollandia since they were getting ready for something big.

First Embarkation Picture

roops destined for service in the Pacific area pass through a portal lending to a ship underneath a sign announcing what they already know and have proved. This scene at San Francisco is the first time in his war that the press has been permitted to inspect and photograph an em

July 1944

Dear Folks,
We made our first port yesterday, and the land really looks good for a change. It's funny tho, not to feel the roll of the ship and feel the pounding of the motor. . . . I can imagine others here, but it seems so very unreal that little me could be way out here miles from home.

We haven't landed yet, but probably will within the next few days. Really, I'm anxious to get started in my work to see what it is like. The Japs aren't too far away from this place, but I don't think there has been an air-raid here from some time. Perhaps they'll let us tell where we are soon. I'm hoping I'll have a chance to visit Australia and New Zealand while down here.

It's rather warm here, even though it's winter! Boy, I'm so messed up on seasons and days that I'm lost! This would really be interesting if it were only a pleasure cruise. We steamed along besides several green islands, passing one native village where a couple of boys were out in a canoe. The harbor here is interesting, . . watching the various ships signal with their blinker lights and mean semaphoring back and forth. All types of craft skim around in the water, now green instead of the ocean blue.

All my love and don't worry too much about me. I'll try to take good care of myself.

James

Dear Mother, Dad, Sister, and Uncle Basil,
That's a rather auspicious heading, isn't it? You probably won't get this until you come back from Camp Meeting, but I just thought you would be having a birthday soon, Mother. Last year I sent you a little brooch, but since we are still aboard ship, I don't have anything to send, and nothing to buy anyway.

As I said, we're still aboard ship, and time has come to mean absolutely nothing. I don't even remember when I wrote you last or what I said, since all my letters are essentially the same as to context, . . what we eat, what we do (nothing), etc.

Try as I may, I just can't seem to think of another thing to say, so I'll close this. Hope your letters come soon, for I would surely like some news of you all.

All my love, and I'll take care of myself,
James

August 11, 1944

Dear Folks,
They tell us it is O.K. to tell that we are in New Guinea, which sounds horrible, but at present, really isn't. The accommodations at this place are excellent, and the chow is especially good--in comparison to that of the boat, excellent! Why, yesterday morning for breakfast we had good hot cakes,

canned butter, syrup, coffee, sausage, & bread & jam. Not bad, eh? Of course we have to use mess kits, and you remember, Dad, what a delightful combination you can get that way. We get lots of bulley beef, but we aren't tired of that yet.

There are four of us in this tent, and we have cots to sleep on. It's cool enough at night for a blanket, so we sleep good, at least. The sun is very hot, and the least effort pops out the sweat. Of course we drink lots of water, and take plenty of salt tablets. The most exasperating things are the sweat running down my glasses and the flies. Honestly, we are as comfortable as in a great navy camp in the states--better than lots. There is a creek to bathe in, and facilities for washing our clothes. I've a bunch of handkerchiefs to wash this afternoon, as well as some clothes. That is one thing I don't like.

More and more I'm appreciating my training at Leonard Wood, for I find such things as rigging, knot tying, will be very practical. I built a rack to tie our packs, etc. on by using lashings they taught me. We also built a wash stand this morning and are planning a shower. We even have running water--of a sort.

So if we stay here a while, we'll have all kinds of contraptions. Seems funny that this was so recently a battlefield, for it's not bad at all.

My time is all mixed up and I can't remember what or when I wrote last, so allow for repetition.

All my love,
James

August 17, 1944

Dear Folks,
We got real ambition the other day and built a shower outside the tent:

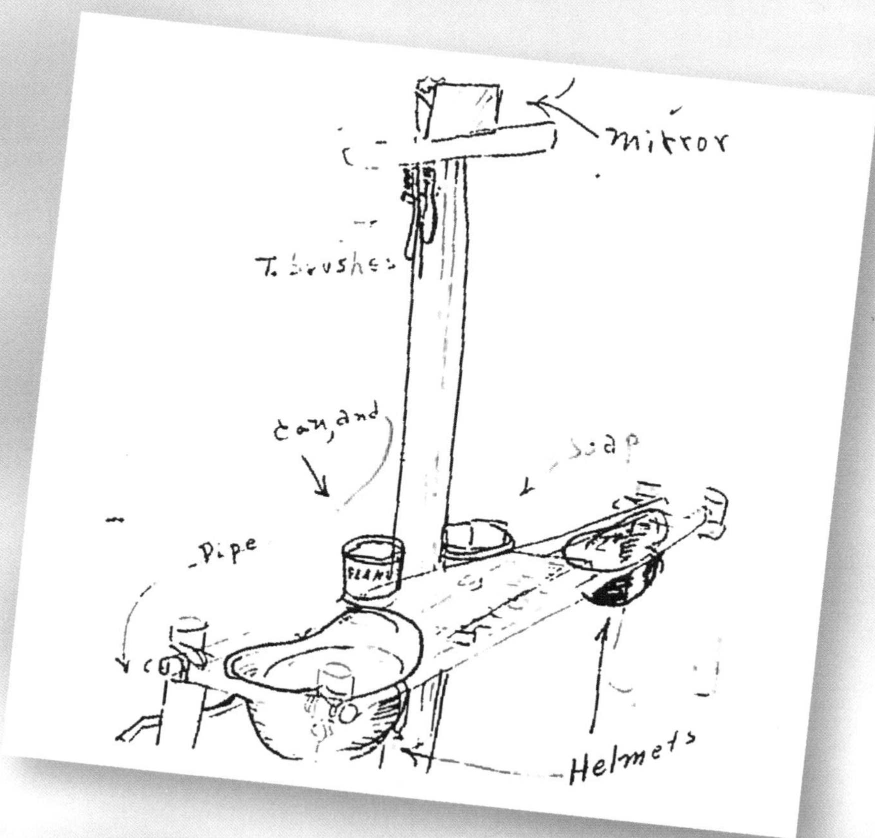

It looks like a Shinto shrine, but works just fine. Soap up on a little platform we built, then pour water in a can with holes in the bottom and clean off. Not too classy, but very effective.

I don't believe I've ever written you of the men with whom I work. Master Sgt. Curt Packard from Arkansas, about 34, is the big chief, then we have 2 T/3's, that's staff with a T in the middle and ranks just below staff. They are Paul Vance, 27 & blond, from Illinois, and Hyman Baras, about 23, tall & gangling, from New York. Our officers are 1st Lt. Miller, a swell man to work with, and 2nd Lt. Rybell, who is rather quiet, but seems to be a good Joe. All in all, we have a swell bunch and get along very well together.

Probably no more of my letters will come through with parts cut. The policy in this area is no cutting--they return any letters which we censored. The Japs are too inquisitive.

We hear Jap propaganda on the radio all the time, and it's better than Bob Hope. They seem to have no conception of our minds, and their attempts are very feeble. We're forbidden to mention any specific item, but they really get some ridiculous stuff to broadcast. Perhaps you can get them shortwave. The bad thing is they jam our own stations from home, so we can't get anything else.

I'm all written out, and it's time for supper.

All my love,
James

August 24, 1944

New Guinea

Dear Folks,
Time goes by so quickly that I'm probably a bit behind with this letter. Ordinarily I wouldn't be writing this right now, but for a little accident.

They've finally got us to working and a rather tough job, too. Our vehicles are here in crates, and our job now is to get them out. Quite a bit of work, too, hacking open those crates.

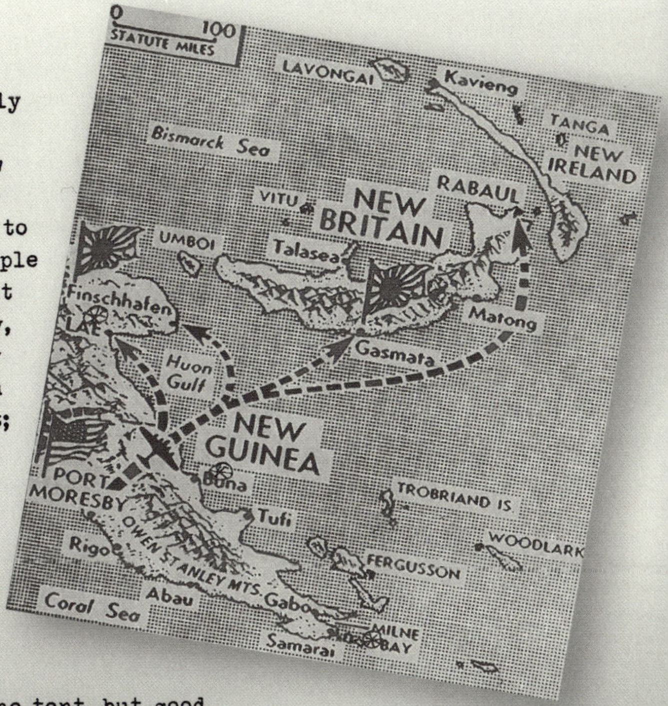

Oh yes! We've lately been introduced to another phase of New Guinea weather--the more moist type. And to prove the first example wasn't pure chance, it did it twice--namely, it rained. And to say "the rains came" is a gross understatement; they came, alright, simply poured, and "having poured, moved on to pour some more!" It made our rains at home look like showers; we had a nice river running alongside the tent, but good ditching kept us dry. The rats became rather panic-stricken, bolted into the tent and squealed back and forth 'till the deluge stopped.

Have I written you about the Owen Stanley mountains. We look right out the door and see them, blue and covered with all kinds of vegetation. There are lots of paw-paw & banana trees, but we haven't had either of those fruits yet. Would you like to have a coconut? Perhaps I can send you one soon. But I was talking of the Owen Stanleys. They are beautiful and high, covered with fleecy clouds. But what a terrific obstacle they must have been to the soldiers who crossed this range from __________ to drive out the Japs. Even in the place I'm in, there are signs of heavy fighting--shot up trees, duds, and pieces of equipment.

We're beginning to get some good rumors and a few ideas as to our dispensation and what our job will be. Perhaps we'll be working very soon. I fear our holiday is all over.

Isn't the news good from Europe? At our present rate, we'll be shoving the Germans down their own chimneys. I see the 36th Div. has been identified as being in Patch's army in S. France. Dad, you should see some of the equipment this man's army has. The Japs just didn't figure what they were up against. One small thing which, I think, is fairly new, is a heater for mess-kit washing water. It's really a little oil or gasoline burner with a stack, the whole of which clamps right on the G.I. cans, and keeps the water boiling hot; there's a round plate which is right down on the bottom of the can & under water which does the trick. That surely beats a wood fire, doesn't it?

Love,
James

August 30, 1944

Dearest Parents and Sister,
I've been working hard to help get the rest of our cars out and a motor pool established. We went for logs yesterday, Mallory, 2 other boys, and I, down the road from Camp to an old abandoned command post. There were dug outs all around, telephone wire, etc., probably American. We loaded one of (the) trucks with logs, to the sound of some outfit firing cannon. Suddenly one of them fired and we heard "swish-swish" of a shell heading for someplace past us, so we pulled our stakes and left!

You'll have to excuse this paper. It's the last 2 sheets I have of this. The stuff on the next sheet is G.I. soap left over from my washing last Sunday. I had a whopper, too. Took me all day, but my clothes came out very nice. It's so very important to keep clean here. The dust is terrific, even a few hours after a hard rain. It gets into everything. I don't believe I've ever had a bath anywhere that was enjoyed as much as the ones we take here. Our shower works very nicely, and in the afternoon, the cool breeze really makes it quite pleasurable. (This soap is ruining my pen!)

What a life. There's nothing much to add that I haven't told you before. As soon as I hear from you, perhaps I can answer some questions. The food is still good, especially after a hard day's work and we all are rapidly getting acclimated to the island. Write whenever you can for letters mean an awful lot more than usual. I'll keep up on mine, too.

All my love,
James

September 4, 1944

Dear Folks,
By this time you've probably, or should have, gotten a number of letters from me, so you're up on general news of this place. But yesterday we really had an interesting day. About a dozen of us got one of the trucks and took off into the jungle. We crawled over rough, mountainous roads some 30 miles to a few native villages. We were quite surprised when a little 10 year old native boy asked our name & address, and wrote his own for us! Of course he was trained by missionaries, who have done excellent work.

What an interesting experience it was, though; if I'd only had a camera. There seems to be no middle aged natives, only children, young people, and old ones, practically all with some type of skin disease. The men are usually very well built,

with high fuzzy hair, dyed a light henna color. Some of them are native policemen and have a special skirt to designate their rank. Many have teeth stained black by beetle nut. The little children are pot-bellied and usually go naked. A few of the women around the mission wore Mother Hubbards, but most have only a skirt; they walk in front of the husband, and carry large loads suspended from their foreheads. A few have tattoos. Most of the men wear only a loin cloth. Some of the ones in the bay area were in paint yesterday--some kind of festival to do with the full moon. They look like a wild lot, but are quite friendly and like Americans very much. Around the villages are a few very spindly, mangy dogs, and offer a couple of pigs. The houses are built on stilts and are a sort of a shed of thatch.

Naturally they all go barefoot, and have tremendous wide feet. They usually don't live past 35, but at that age, look to be 65. This place was way back in the jungle and we saw what that looks like, increasing our respect for the men who fought here.

There are all kinds of trees, ferns, vines and other underbrush as well as kunai grass in there. And they say there's gold, too. Some fellows digging a well near here found a few flecks, but don't want to stay to pan it. Rather go home; I guess.

You said that the censor had cut out some things from my letters, what I don't know. Sometimes they go out of their way to do that, it seems, but it's a pretty big responsibility.

I'll write weekly, at least (if I can keep up with the days) and unless a letter is delayed, you should hear that often. Your air mail gets here pretty well, but it seems a long time between letters.

I can't think of anything else right now, so I'll say good-night. My regards to everyone.

Love,
James

September 25, 1945

Dear Folks,
What would you think if I decided to stay in New Guinea after the war?! Last week a "Lt. Dawsett" of the Australian army gave us a lecture on jungle fighting and orientation on N. Guinea. He is over 50, but doesn't look a day over 30, and is in excellent physical condition; he has 7 samurai swords which he took personally and has fought in the last war, in Africa and Crete, and nearly all the fights out here. He gave some very interesting information on New Guinea. It is very rich in minerals of all kinds and in forests, but is very undeveloped. Plantations of pineapples, coconuts, bananas and cocoa thrive, and there is good ranching land. Proper breeding eliminates ticks in the cattle. Lease on 2,000 acres is $0.00 for the 1st 10 years and 3d (3 pence - 4--) per acre for the next 10. Now that the army has built roads, and will undoubtedly leave much motor equipment here, development should be greatly aided. I've written for information on the subject and am going to see what the drawbacks are. Lt. Dawsett has a cocoa plantation near Rabaul and says he never cleared less than $10,000.00 per year. There should be lots of chances in many fields, from gold mining to farming. 3 or 4 crops of pineapples can be produced a year, with a tremendous production per acre. If a cannery were established, it

should be a lucrative trade, using the natives for labor. I'll let you know what I find out. There are also many birds of paradise back in the mts. and you know what they sell for.

Love,
James

P.S. It's beginning to rain again. Been doing that all week.

October 1st, 1944

Dear Folks,

Our team and Mallory's went out last week and fired on a range. There was a battle sitting on a post about 50 or so yards away, which I broke with the first shot! Then we shot up a few tin cans and had a lot of fun, but my beginner's luck was over and I only shot about average. I'm glad we have that machine gun, especially if we get in close-in fighting. That has a tremendous firepower.

We had K-ration along for a picnic lunch and it was very good. It comes in cardboard boxes, dinner, supper, breakfast separately. Breakfast has coffee, bacon and eggs, fruit bar; dinner, --cheese and ham, cigarettes, chocolate bar, lemonade; supper- potted pork loaf, caramels, agarettes, cocoa, boulbon and all have biscuits of wheat, etc. It's really a good ration and much better than C ration. Though we fished all day, we didn't catch a thing. The crayfish eat up all the bait. One fellow was using hand grenades, and we managed to get a couple of mess kits full of small fish, which we fried. They were good. They got 2 fish about a foot long, which were very nice, bass, I think. The grenade stuns them and makes them easy to catch.

Dad, sometime when you are in the mood or something I write reminds you of some of your army experiences, write me some of them. I guess you had all this army stuff (mild word) to put up with, too. I'm beginning to think civilian life would be nice for a change. However, in my estimation, it's going to be a long time yet. These Jap people are really dug in and each individual fox hole, bunker, and dug out has to be cleaned out separately, by flame thrower or grenade. If people had an idea of what the men are up against here and will hit in the Philippines; the country would have a more serious outlook. It's easy to watch developments on a map. It looks so simple. Most of their equipment is comparable to ours, and the individual soldier is a tricky, mean, and fanatical opponent. Have talked to lots of fellows who've seen action and it's a grim story. We'll beat them, but it won't be easy.

We still haven't shipped so I'll be missing your letters before long, I guess.

All my love,
James

Leyte, 1944

Air Corps studying aerial pictures, similar to what we did on Photo Interpretation teams.

We got to Hollandia on Monday October 9th and left the following Friday, October 13th for the invasion of Leyte, Philippine Islands! We reported in but no one knew what to do with us or what we could do because we were such a new specialty. At the landing area we had our Photo Interpretation kit with stereo glasses, scales, etc., so we went out under a tree and began to study the pictures. There was an obvious zigzag trap dug parallel to and a couple of hundred feet inland from the beach, but most of the area was thickly covered with palm trees, making it impossible to see through to the ground. Our A-Day objective was Hill 522, which commanded the beach area, a short way inland and adjacent to the little village or barrio of Palo. We could identify many signs of digging on it, but nothing major. Then something happened that really made our reputation and gained us great credibility for the rest of the war.

We were shown on the photos the area that the G-1 Colonel, Tom Comprere, had picked out for our Division Command Post. As we studied the photos, we were convinced that this was a swamp! We had just arrived fresh from the States, we were a totally unknown factor, and all the commanders had been advised of this location. Was it too late to make changes? We looked and looked at the pictures. Finally, Lieutenant Miller asked each of us if we were sure, and on our affirmation, he went after Colonel Compere, who shortly joined us. Fortunately, we were finally able to persuade him that we were right, and he reluctantly agreed to change to another area we picked out. There is no way to express how relieved we were after the landing to find that we were correct, that the first area was truly a swamp, and we had prevented a major problem!

At the 1989 reunion of the 24th Division in Fort Worth, I visited with Tom Compere and told him how fearful we had been that we had made a mistake and that we were more afraid of him than of the Japs! He told me that after the landing he had waded out chest deep in that area! It truly was a swamp and he had had to put people on duty there to forward messengers to the correct command post location.

Movie actor Lew Ayers

Of course, we had no time to learn anything about Hollandia or see much of it. Things were in a big hustle getting ready to leave. I went to Supply and drew an M-1 rifle because I was more comfortable with it than with the machine gun we were issued. Quickly the time came for us to leave and we boarded the USS *John S. Land* and joined the convoy.

We staged from Hollandia and met the other divisions at sea. The 1st Cavalry staged from the Adiralties, and the 7th and 96th from Kwjalien and Honolulu, I think. The 7th had been in combat in the Aleutians and on Kwajalien, but the 96th had not seen combat. Somehow all of that got together out in the middle of the ocean and headed for Leyte.

The armada was huge! I think our ship was pretty well in the center of the convoy because we had the Philippine President, Sergio Osmena, and his Chief of Staff, Carlos Romulo, both of whom we would see daily, on board the ship. We could not see the end of ships in any direction. There were six battle ships, eighteen escort carriers, eight cruisers, thirty destroyers, and hundreds of other crafts of all kinds from troop ships to landing ship, tanks (LSTs), landing craft infantries (LCIs), and nearly anything else that would float. It was probably the largest such force in history. It really staggers the imagination to think how anyone could plan and control such an immense project. The sight was awesome, and it is doubtful that its like will ever be seen again.

We were lucky in being on a larger ship. We had good quarters, did not roll and pitch as the smaller ships did, and had a good mess. We were much more comfortable, and we felt much safer, too. On board our ship was the movie actor Lew Ayres. He was a conscientious objector but was serving as a medical corpsman with our division. He had starred in one of the first major sound movies, *All's Quiet on the Western Front*, a powerful pacifist story about World War I, and we would see him on deck nearly every day.

Our trip was uneventful. We spent time up on deck watching the other ships, playing cards, writing letters, sharpening our machetes, cleaning our rifles, reading, or going over our instructions for the landing. And doing lots of thinking! My twenty-first birthday came on October 18, just two days out of Leyte, and I wondered if it would be my last! We did have ice cream that day, and a welcome treat it was.

Now there was nothing to do but what soldiers to the most of . . . wait!

A-Day, October 20, 1944, dawned clear and hot, very hot! We had been awoken early, and then had the usual army wait until our appointed time. The plan was that planes would bomb the assault beaches with napalm—a mixture of oil and liquid rubber—but from our ship we could see no planes at all. There was a battleship between us and the beach slowly cruising along and shelling the shore and Hill 522—our A-Day objective. Their big guns made a most distinctive sound, a *CA-RUMPH*—totally different from any other artillery I have ever heard. We could not see any return fire from the shore, but inland to our right was a column of black smoke slowly going nearly straight up. The bay was full of hundreds of ships and boats of all kinds.

Soon it was our time to load up! There was a rope net hung over the side of the ship and we had to climb down that into a waiting landing craft-vehicle personnel (LCVP) bobbing alongside. That is not as easy as it may sound. I had on my fully loaded backpack, full ammunition belt, M-1 rifle, helmet, gas mask, canteen, and inflatable life belt. A slip and I would likely have fallen between the ship and the LCVP and sunk like a rock! It was a mixed blessing to arrive safely in the landing craft, which was soon to be on its way to a hotly contested landing! It was around 10:00 AM.

I have forgotten what wave we were in, but I think around the 18th. Packard, Miller, and I were assigned to different landing crafts. On mine was Sergeant Don Twining from the G-2 Order of Battle Team. Also aboard was a naval lieutenant named Ryder, a bomb disposal officer assigned to our division for this operation who stood up at the front where he could watch for mines. Later at the invasion of Mindoro he would lose an eye when a Kamikaze plane hit the ship he was on, and still later we would see in *Time* magazine where he defused the mines on the Pasig River Bridge when the 1st Cavalry Division went into Manila. We circled a while and then it was time for us to go in.

There was a jeep and trailer on our craft, and as we neared the landing, the order was given to start it. But it wouldn't start! The solider in charge tried and tried but with no luck. Suddenly we felt the jolt of running aground in the shallow water, the ramp dropped, and the cox'n sitting totally exposed on the rear of the landing craft told us in no uncertain terms to get that jeep out of his boat! We pushed it out, jumped in beside it, and waded ashore in hip deep water, while he backed out and headed out to sea to bring in more troops. So far, so good.

As we came out of the water we saw soldiers scattered all around, clutching their weapons, seeking cover among the downed palm trees and hugging the ground. No one was moving. One fellow was on his face with a hole in the back of his helmet, the result of a Jap mortar shell that had hit just moments before. We did not know it at the time, but there were none of our troops in front of these . . . just Japs!

The Division Command Post was supposed to be south or down the beach from where we landed, so Don and I started walking that way. It was blistering hot. We sat down on a palm log, took one of the numerous green coconuts that littered the area, and cut it open to drink. As we sat there, some fellows came running up about 100 feet behind us, set up a mortar, and began firing! I told Don we better move on because it would draw fire. His comment was, "Draw fire, hell! Look at the trajectory." The thing was pointed almost straight up! About then we saw two fellows packing a third whose foot was covered with a bloody bandage. We decided it was time to move on!

The beach was chaotic. Everyone was searching for their unit and trying to get organized. Jeeps, weapons carriers, and tanks were milling around and more were coming ashore rapidly. The whole area was covered with downed palm trees from the shelling. We soon ran into a real mess. The Japs had built four bunkers side by side, made out of coconut logs set upright in the ground in two parallel rows several feet apart, with the space between filled with dirt. They were armed with 75-mm guns, and among other things, had knocked out an LST as it landed. One of the bunkers had been blown up, another was in the process of being covered up with sand by an armored bulldozer, and the other two were under siege. That's where we saw our first dead Japs.

The existence of these bunkers was a tragedy. After we got up the Leyte Valley to Jaro, the G-2 people brought us another set of photos of Red Beach that they had just unpacked, taken a week or so after the ones we had been given at Hollandia. During that interim, lanes of fire had been cut in the undergrowth, making *V*'s, which pointed directly at each of the bunkers. No one was trained to pick up this clue until we came, but if we had had those pictures in time, we would have easily made the identification and they would have been destroyed before the landing.

We circled around behind the bunkers and went on our way. We found our command post about midafternoon and discovered that Packard and Miller were both safe and sound, as were Lieutenant Stewart and Jack Waltz, Don's other Order of Battle team members. Packard had a narrow escape when a shrapnel-damaged palm tree collapsed and a large section of it almost fell on him. He was able to scramble out of the way just in the nick of time and only had a slightly bruised leg. We spent an uneasy and spooky night in our holes, swatting mosquitos and waiting for daylight.

Breakfast the next morning was interesting! Our cooks had two small stoves sitting out in the open in the middle of our camp. We took turns lining up to eat, three or four at a time to make a smaller target. When my turn came, we suddenly heard gunfire, and I looked up in time to see a burning Jap plane going down close at hand; the fellows in the other line had a 20-mm shell come down and bury itself in the mud without exploding! It all happened in just a moment, and I stood there with my mess kit in my hand and wondered "what am I doing here?"

We had a funny incident later that day. We needed drinking water, so we took our water can and went back to the beach area where the engineers had set up a water point. This was a portable canvas tank, 10 or 12 feet in diameter, fed through a hose from a shallow hole dug in the ground. The water was heavily chlorinated, so we decided to go out on the disabled LST and get fresh water. Suddenly we heard the distinctive sound of shots from a Jap 22-mm rifle! We were right by a knocked-out amphibious tank called an *alligator*, partly in the surf. Everyone was diving for cover, so we quickly scrambled along one side of the alligator. Cautiously I peered around the end of the machine to be faced with another soldier peering in my direction with equal caution from the other side. We both laughed when we realized that one of us just had to be wrong! The peril was quickly eliminated when someone used a Thompson submachine gun to send the sniper to join his honorable ancestors.

We moved our command post that afternoon to get further away from the beach area and closer to the action. As several of us were moving up, we met some fellows who had a Jap prisoner. They gave him to us to take on to the new command post, so our interrogators, who were American Japs (Nisei), could question him. These Nisei were brave men and worked at least as far down as battalion level. Sergeant Kenny Shimbo is the only one whose name I remember now. Prisoners were a treasure. Because of their own fanaticism, they would not usually surrender. And our troops hated them so badly, they often would not take prisoners. This one appeared to be young, was wearing only a breech cloth, and was understandably nervous. He fell in behind me, so I undid my belt and moved my knife from the back to the front, just in case. But there was no trouble and we delivered him safely.

Late that afternoon Miller, Packard, and I dug a three-man hole in a T shape in a former pig pen! Shortly before dusk there was some shooting and we quickly dove into our hole. The bullets were going right over us with that distinctive snapping sound! The shots sounded like our own weapons, but we never found out what happened. We took some of the sheet iron that had been the pig's covering and made a roof over our hole to protect against the inevitable rain. Such luxury! Unfortunately the tin seemed to magnify sounds, and the buzzing of the mosquitos was tremendously enhanced all night. We would smear on mosquito repellent, go to sleep, wake up in a couple of hours getting bit, rub on some more repellent, and try to go back to sleep. It was quiet except for the sound of our artillery firing harassing fire throughout the night.

It is impossible at this point in time to remember details in proper sequence, but these random items are memories of things that happened before we moved up through Palo.

- Several of the Philippine guerillas came to our command post. Most were real patriots and heroes, but a few were hardly more than outlaws. They were excellent sources of intelligence for us. These groups had even printed their own currency during the Jap occupation and I brought home several examples.
- On the day we landed, Don and I were walking up the beach when we saw several cases of Jap beer stacked next to a nipa hut. Although there were many people around, true to our training, no one had touched them. It was such an obvious booby trap. Then along came a couple of fellows in a weapons carrier who stopped, got out, loaded the beer on the back of the vehicle, and drove off! There was no problem at all!
- Leyte was a sea of mud! We slept in it, ate it, waded through it, and dug trucks out of it. Staying clean was impossible. But it was amazing to see the natives dressed in white shirts and pants, with the pants rolled up a bit, and the women in white dresses, all barefooted, going to church, spotlessly clean! We never could figure out how they did it.
- We could trade atabrine tablets, undershirts, or cigarettes with the native women to wash our clothes—a wonderful exchange. They would take the laundry to the nearest stream, soap everything, then lay the items on a rock and beat them vigorously with a wooden paddle, followed by a good rinsing. We also traded for chickens, eggs, bananas, camotes, and other food items. Mother sent me some sewing machine needles, which

were great trading material. It seemed that every little nipa hut had a foot-powered Singer sewing machine in it, and of course, the people had not been able to get needles for a long time.

- There were two major Japanese attacks on Palo, the second on the night of October 24th. The Japs herded a group of Filipinos in front of them and were able to get the jump on our people. One objective was the bridge, and that is where Maas was killed. A number of division headquarter people were in Palo, and several told us of their experiences. It was sheer bedlam! One counterintelligence fellow told of being upstairs in a building, prone on the floor. Japs came in downstairs and shot through the ceiling. One bullet came almost all the way through the floor right under him! Another friend, Carter, a combat MP, was dug in under a building (most buildings are up on stilts) and saw and participated in all of it. The Japs captured one of our machine guns, which they set up in the town square. In the dark, nobody knew who was who, and it was about two hours before our people could regain control. Our division command post was less than a mile from Palo that night.
- We got our first run of aerial photos about this time, but they were not much help. They were flown at 50,000 feet, too small a scale to be of tactical use. Even though the landing strips at Tacloban and Dulag had been captured, it would be a couple of weeks before the engineers could get them operational, so we had no land-based planes. These pictures came from the St. Lo, a baby flat top, which was sunk on October 25 in the Battle of Leyte Gulf by one of the first Kamikaze attacks of the war. We were not aware of this battle taking place until it was over. Later we talked to some of our division who were on Suluan and Homonhan Islands and who were eyewitnesses. They said it was awesome! We had a close call, and if the Jap navy had kept it coming, I supposed I would still be on Leyte!
- Palo is at the foot of Leyte Valley, a broad flat area, bounded on the west by a ridge of mountains running north and south, and on the east by some hills that parallel the shore line of Leyte Gulf. The valley is covered with rice paddies, palm and bamboo groves, cogon grass, and jungle. There is only one narrow dirt road running north from Palo through Jaro to Carigara. We were told the land was owned largely by nonresidents. The people we saw were poor and had been badly treated by the Japanese. They were overjoyed to see us.

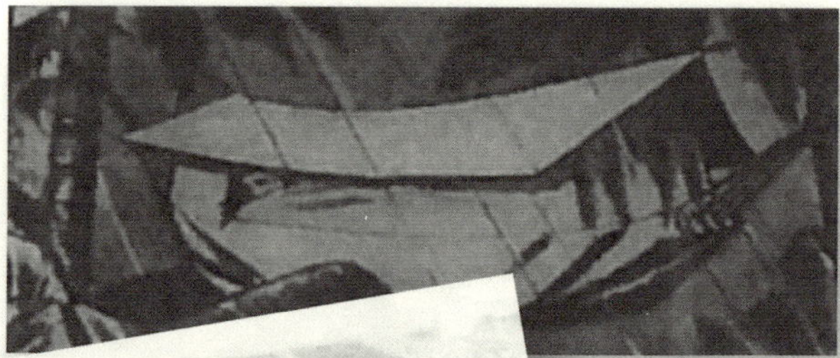

Jungle hammock

Philippine houses near Jaro, Leyte

Our next command post was just north of Palo. There I acquired my own strieker, Tote. He was about nine, washed my clothes and took care of me. His sister started teaching us Visayan, which has many Spanish words. Unfortunately this only lasted a few days before we moved on. We were invited by some of the locals to a meal, but we were afraid to eat much of it because of sanitation reasons. I am sure we must have hurt their feelings.

Our artillery fired intermittent harassing fire at the Japs all night. We would hear the sound of canon fire, then the swish as the shells went over, soon followed by explosions as they landed far up ahead. One night we were in our foxholes nearly asleep when a couple of shells went over. It was quiet. Then softly a voice spoke out, "just keep going, Big Boy!" It broke up the whole camp!

Then we had a typhoon. How did it rain! I was in my jungle hammock and by pulling one side down could keep the rain off. But then I realized as I dozed off, the side would flop up and the wind would blow the rain all over me. Packard was trying to sleep in his foxhole. His head was out and only the tips of his toes were showing above the water that filled the hole! We were like a bunch of drowned rats. The next morning, Rybel, Vance, and Baras were on a ship in Leyte Gulf during the storm and when they joined us with all the equipment a few days later they told us how frightened they were as the ships banged together. Maybe we had the best of it after all.

In a few days we were in the barrio of Jaro. We set up our truck, fly, jeep, and trailer a couple of blocks from the center of the little town. We had saved a tin of tropical butter, jelly, and other goodies from our 10-in-1 rations and had traded for three chickens, so we decided to have a feast. One chicken escaped and was last seen flying over some of the nipa houses, chased by several Filipino urchins. We were never to see either again! Miller had us boil the chicken first to tenderize it. Then we proposed to fry it in the carefully saved butter. But the butter would not melt, even directly over the fire of our Coleman stove! So we went to the mess tent for grease, then fried our chicken and some thinly sliced camotes, added some local fruit, and at last served dinner. (The chicken was still tough!)

One night almost at dusk we suddenly heard planes and looked up to see several transports, flying almost on the deck! It was instantaneous. They had come and gone before we realized what was happening. We found out later that these were four Jap planes loaded with raiders whose mission was to land on Barauen airstrip south of us and disable it. They missed the target and were eliminated within a few days. But they were followed within a week by a full attack of several hundred Jap paratroopers, who created a real battle. We were glad they were not in our area!

One of our command posts was in a palm grove north of Jaro, a place we used a second time after the division was relieved at Breakneck Ridge. There we slept on cots in pyramidal tents, and even set up the hot shower unit someone had "liberated" from the navy back at Hollandia. One of our G-2 sergeants was named Mario Bigi, a tall Italian fellow with a big handlebar mustache, so we called our G-2 area "Mario's Barrio."

Three G2 Clerks with our division. Fred Goettinger, Al Paulos, and Bartow Tomlin

See story on page 64.

Bamboo grows in thickets and may be were four to six inches in diameter. We used it to make racks over our cots to hold our mosquito bars, sidewalks to get out of the mud, tent framing, and other things. One day Vance and I took the jeep and went back a few miles to cut some. As we walked from the jeep with our machetes in hand. Vance suddenly slipped on the slick mud and fell, cutting all four fingers of one hand to the bone! I took him to the field hospital near our command post, which sent him to a hospital clear back on Guadalcanal, and it was several weeks before he rejoined us.

At night it was the duty of the defense platoon to set up a perimeter around the command post for protection. One night I pulled guard duty with a G-2 corporal named Goettinger from Pleasanton, New York. We were in the foxhole together trying to stay awake, alert to hear every little sound. It was nearing daylight, and we thought we could see something just a few yards in front of us! We strained to see, and sure enough, there was enough light to make out the crouching figure of . . . a Philippine woman! Then she spoke, "Sair, do you have any dirrrrty clothes to wash today?" She knew exactly where we were even in the dark, but we had no idea how she got there or how long she had been there. We had neither seen nor heard anything. I suppose she could just as easily have been a Jap!

The action moved on up through Carigara, turned westward along the coast, and started down Ormoc Valley. The Japs had decided to make an all-out effort to stop us on Leyte and were bringing in many reinforcements. We hit them at Breakneck and Kilay Ridges. The map showed up at this point a loop in the road that measured a mile across, but we could not find this extremely prominent place on our photos. Miller drove up to the headquarters of X Corps Artillery and visited with Captain Hervey, OIC of their Photo Interpretation Team. They had the same problem, so Hervey got in their spotter plane and flew over the area and discovered that the map was wrong! There was no loop, just a wiggly road going through a pass between the ridges.

We soon moved the command post through Carigara and on to a spot called Pinamapoan. This required us to keep one command post going until the forward one would get moved and communication established, and I stayed with the group at the old one. Sometime after dark we got the word that the new one was in operation and we shut down. A storm had blown in and we stayed up nearly all night in the blackout tent playing bridge, trying to stay dry. We would hear the wind coming and everyone would grab hold of the tent to keep it from blowing away. It was a wild and wet night.

Shortly we made our last move forward to a spot called Capoocan. The road along this area was unstable and was soon totally impassable, and the division was in trouble for lack of supplies. Air drops were used but often the supplies ended up in Jap hands. They even captured one of the Red Cross trucks. Dukws were also used to ferry around the road. This command post was a spooky one, with the ocean on one side, and high jungle covered bluffs on the other, and the Japs only a few miles away. We were vulnerable. On Christmas Eve, we were playing bridge in the blackout tent when a Washing Machine

Charley came over. We ran out and jumped into our fox holes, but he flew off, so we went back inside the tent. Soon he was back, so we went back to the hole. This happened several times as he flew up and down the beach buzzing like a fly, and finally dropped his bombs a mile or so away. He probably had information as to our whereabouts, but fortunately did not find us.

I got sick with dysentery and was sent back to Carigara to the hospital. I went by Dukw. We had several Jap prisoners who nearly collapsed when we drove out into the ocean and became water borne. They were so impressed with the amphibious vehicle that they told the interpreter they wanted to join up with us! The hospital was set up in the village school building where I stayed about a week. One night we were sleeping peacefully when all kinds of weapons began to go off! In an instant everybody rolled off their cots to the floor. Surely we were under attack! But it was only a celebration for the advent of the new year—1945! Fortunately my sickness was quickly over, and I rejoined the division right after New Year's Day.

Our division was relieved about this time, and we pulled out and back to the command post north of Jaro, which we had used before. Some elements were detached and used in the invasion of Mindoro, but we were not part of that operation as a division.

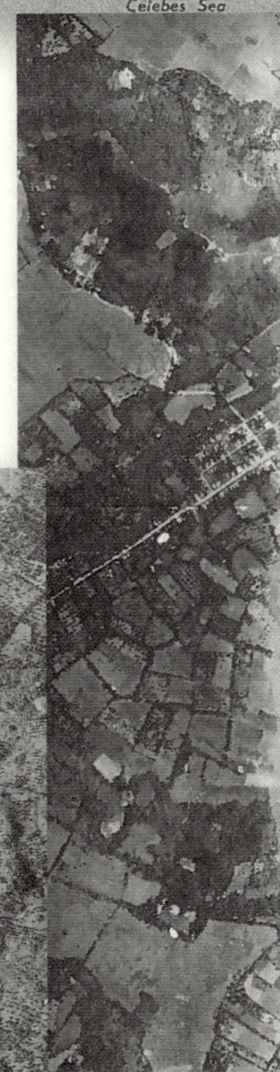

Aerial views of Leyte

It was good to be back in our old command post. We enjoyed movies at night and had a sense of safety, not always justified, however! One night all the lights were on, the movies were showing, everyone was relaxed, when all at once, W*HAM! WHAM! WHAM! WHAM! WHAM!* Everyone hit the dirt! I was in the G-2 tent reading so I dove into the shallow drainage ditch around the tent, and I think I got all the way down in it. It was chaos at the movies, with people running over each other, into trees, getting hit with flashlights, or whatever as all the lights were doused and everyone sought cover. Rybel dove under our trucks, forgetting that we had dug holes for the wheels. He got a bad cut on the scalp. The doctor had to shave around it, making him look like a monk, so to his annoyance we called him "Father Rybel." We had about thirty casualties of various kinds. The 26th Division command post was about three miles south of us, and they had the same experience, the explosions seeming to be between us. We never learned the source.

This was the only place that I went on patrol. One morning several of us went out with one of the sergeants of headquarter company, whose nervousness and agitation inspired no comfort. I was on point as we took off down a path through the high cogon grass. Our mission was to see if there were any Jap stragglers or patrols about. We had gone a mile or so, every sense alert, careful at every turn when sud-

Various invasion pictures, Red Beach, Leyte, October 20, 1944

denly I fell into a hole. It was several feet deep and I have no idea why it was there. Fortunately it was not lined with sharpened bamboo stakes, as they sometimes were. We found nothing so returned safely to the command post.

About midmorning another day we heard rifle shots close to the command post. We grabbed our guns and hurried to see what was going on. We found a soldier who had killed a Jap lieutenant and two enlisted men and whose stripped bodies he was in the process of burying in a shell hole. I brought home a photo of a young Japanese woman taken from the dead lieutenant's billfold. I've often wondered who she was (see picture on page 62).

Another morning a clerk was outside the G-3 tent, posting his map, which was propped up on an ammo case leaning against a tent pole. He dropped his crayon, and as he leaned over to pick it up, a bullet hit the map board just where he had been sitting! He was white as a sheet at the narrow escape. Two weeks later he died . . . from spinal meningitis!

Our time on Leyte was at an end. We loaded our truck and trailer and pulled out for Red Beach. It had changed so much since our landing that we could not recognize anything! The bulldozers had pushed up dirt ramps out to the LSTs. I was the first one to load up on our ship, so I backed the truck and trailer all the way down the ramp, up into the LST and clear to the stern on the first try! I decided that I had really arrived as a truck driver.

Here are some random comments and memories of Leyte.

- The first afternoon of the invasion after we had found the division command post, Packard made some coffee in his helmet over a little fire.

Invasion pictures, Leyte

This practice was strongly discouraged because the heat takes the temper out of the metal. Also, as we found to our disgust, the first batch can't be drunk because the heat also releases the olive drab paint on the inside of the iron hat! The second batch wasn't too bad, however.

- Pervading everything was the mud and the heat. We invaded during the rainy season, and all the islands are volcanic with powdery soil, and a little water makes a real loblolly in a hurry. It rained every afternoon, but within an hour or so the roads were dusty, thanks to the blistering tropic sun.
- Then there were the insects—all bigger than life and all of them biters! Lots of big mosquitos, spiders as large as your hand, huge centipedes, and countless others. There was a Lieutenant Wheeler in G-2, an Aggie, who got bit by a centipede one night and from the size of the bite marks we all wondered if perhaps it was a snakebite. Our jungle hammocks were really great when we were able to use them because of their built in mosquito netting.
- One of our pieces of equipment was a compact photo developing kit, housed in a trunk like box about three-feet square. The idea was for us to take ground shots of various things that we had detected in aerial photos and send both back to Camp Ritchie for training purposes. The only flaw was that we had no training at all in how to develop and print pictures! Miller knew as little as did Packard and I, but not enough to do the job right. Fortunately, Master Sergeant Minor White, the ranking noncommissioned officer of the G-2 section, had been a professional photographer in civilian life, and he became our instructor. We set up the unit in the truck but had to wait until about 11:00 at night for water to get cool enough not to run the emulsion. White became quite well known after the war for his photographic art. We were surprised to find that he was a homosexual and much of his work was salacious.

October 26, 1944

Dear Folks,
It's been some time since I've had a letter from you, but as you've seen in the papers, we are in the Philippines now. About the place, all I can say is what doesn't crawl, hops, what doesn't hop, flies, and everything bites! Mosquitas are so thick, you can't stir them, and chicken wire makes a good net to keep them out. I don't believe they've had a good square meal until we arrived.

I can't tell you not to worry about me, for I know you will. They don't play for fun here, but I'll try to take good care of myself. So far, the only Japs I've seen have been dead ones and prisoners, but they were only a few hundred yards away when we hit the beach. We have had air raids, and rain every night; a fox hole isn't the best place to sleep, but we're making out O.K.! Snipers take pot shots at us once in a while, but they rather quickly find themselves full of lead.

We've eaten pretty well so far. There is a "10 and 1" rations, which have some of the best cheese, jelly, butter(!), corn, good things. Not like fried chicken, though.

Perhaps I can tell you a little about the Philippines. It's much like the rest of S. Pacific area --jungles, coconut palms, mud, which is quite gummy and very slick, bamboo, and lots of good hot sun. The Philippines are very glad to see us and tell stories of the usual Jap management. It's surprising how much, and what odd shaped bundles the natives can carry on their heads. And there are lots of water buffalo and bamboo huts just like you see in pictures.

Packard cuts Mims' hair

We have about as good a set up as we could have. It gets awfully monotonous, digging fox holes every time we move up, but they are quite comforting when bombers come over or snipers get ambitious. I believe I'll be heartily sick of the Islands after I've dug holes all the way across them.

It was quite an experience coming in on A day, but it seemed I should be seeing it in a newsreel rather than being there. We had to wade a few feet, filling our shoes with water, of course. We were awfully thirsty and chopped open some green coconuts, which are mostly juice. You can't imagine the confusion of the beach. It seems impossible that anything can get organized, but it does. And very quickly all kinds of stuff starts moving up and is getting in shape to function.

There's not much I can write without including military information. Mother, you are a good one to save things, so how about saving items about our division and any pictures from the paper. Maybe I can tell you something about them when I come home.

All my love,
James

November 6, 1944

Dear Mother and Dad,
You said you hoped we'd had rain. Well it's just as dusty on the roads as N.G. but we did have rain--a typhoon, in fact. I was sleeping in my hammock and kept dry, though I rocked around and nearly turned over. But my fox hole and my shoes were both full of water.

Although news reports give our unit location on the Island, I can't tell you exactly where I am. See by reading the papers, you can find the towns we've occupied, and figure that if I'm not there, I probably might have been, maybe, or was possibly. I'll have to give you an orientation on New Guinea and the Philippines when I get back.

I got quite sick the other day. It was very hot and I drank a lot of water without thinking. So consequently, I

was very sick at my stomach! Got cleaned out good, and was O.K. next day, I threw-up when I was empty. First time I've been sick like that in a very long time--since I was small, in fact. You remember those bilious attacks I used to have. Would have been nearly pleasant to have been sick at home 'cause you'll have been there to take care of me, Mom! And get ice cream and cold drinks the next day. Am feeling as usual, now.

Well, this place is still full of coconuts and us! Have been trying to get some roasting ears but no luck yet. The Japs took practically everything from the natives--even their clothes, and they need everything we can give them and what they already have for food.

All my love,
James

P.S. Packard gave me a hair cut the other day. He wasn't cut out to be a barber. If you find a small pair of clippers, send them. Did you ever get the necklace and bracelets?

Nov. 10, 1944

My dearest Sis,
Your birthday card and that scuh-rewey letter in which Alberta stuck some sort of amendment have reached me "somewhere in the Philippines." No doubt you can easily figure out from the news reports where the 24th Div. is, but I'm just "somewhere!" I won't repeat the first letter I wrote from here since Mother probably sent you that. About all I can say is it seems I should be seeing it in a newsreel instead of in person.

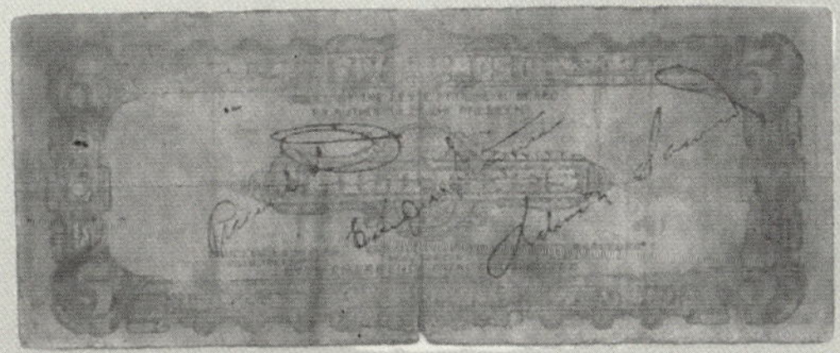

We had quite a treat for breakfast today. We have had our kitchen with us for some time, but naturally we don't have fresh food--all from cans. One of the ready-to-eat rations we had the first few days had a can of bacon in it, which we saved. Yesterday I traded a Philippine boy one of my undershirts for 7 (seven) (siete) eggs -- slightly

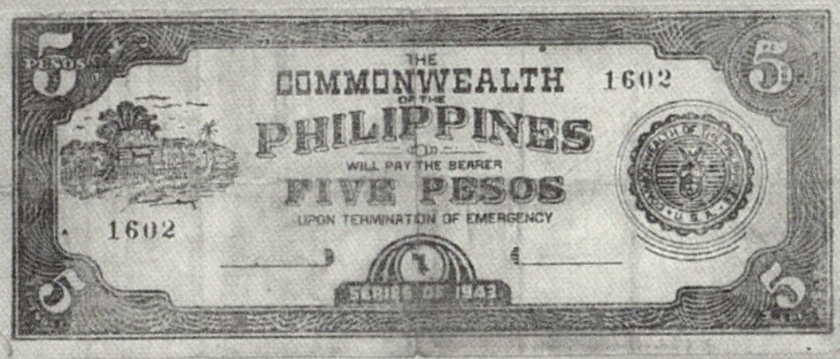

Philippine money issued by the Japanese during occupation

fertile. We have a little gasoline stove, so guess what I had for breakfast? Bacon and eggs! And very good, too. Perhaps that doesn't sound so wonderful, but it's certainly a welcome change.

Hope to acquire a chicken soon. Would have earlier, but don't know how to dress the darn thing. Quite a few of the various fellows have had some fried chicken, which would be darn nice, wouldn't it?

I'm sending you a couple of Jap examples of Philippine money. Don't know what you can do with it, but I'll send it.

All my love,
James

19 Nov. 1944

Dear Folks,
Things rather quiet so I got started on this letter. You know, I have to really rack the old brain to think of anything to write. The army suggests we say "the chow is good; I feel fine, and all my love," and that's about how it sums up.

As for chow, by some miracle we had fresh fried eggs for breakfast the other morning. They were delicious. We are trying to encourage our two chickens to come through, but this unsettled life rather upsets them. Looks like they're headed for the frying pan!

Honestly I can squeeze out another line. Lt. Miller is putting some kind of vegetable to cooking. They taste like very dry sweet potatoes.

All my love,
James

November 21, 1944

Didn't get this mailed so I'll add a few lines, and a couple of pieces of Jap money to put in my scrap book.

Philippine women do the laundry

The chickens' doom has been sealed. They are now destined to provide a rather large Thanksgiving dinner, supplemented by whatever else we can beg, borrow, or requisition by moonlight. Bet you wish you could be here.

Was just eating a piece of S. Pacific cake--coconut. Very good and fresh. If you'd like one, I'll send it, probably after the 1st of the year when mail isn't too clogged. They'll make very good cake, but they are a little hard to open.

I think my war bonds have been canceled. Don't worry if they don't come and I'll straighten it out. I'll really have a lot of money (3 months when I get paid!)

I'll close this time, am running out of paper.

Love,
James
P.S. This place is VERY wet!

November 26, 1944
Philippine Islands

Dear Mother and Dad,
Well, there are lots of things I'd like to write you, but practically everything reflects on something which would be valuable to the enemy. However, since this is the rainy season I'll leave it to you to imagine that we've been rather wet! Perhaps newsreels and newspapers give you an

idea. I don't do my washing now--the Filipinas do it for "a shirt, food, or most anything." It's hard to dry, for the Sun isn't out a lot. And, too, we're naturally on the move a lot, which makes it hard to keep everything in order.

Well, on Thanksgiving/23rd we did have fresh turkey! Our cooks are excellent, and I've not eaten turkey cooked any better except at home. Don't know how they did so well in a field kitchen. I was lucky, too. Ours was on the 23rd (Nov.) for supper, and the next day I had to drive to another place and ate dinner there. Luckily they had their turkey then, so through no conniving of mine I received a double blessing to be doubly thankful for! Went to the service Thanksgiving

114th Photo Interpretation (PI) Team: Lt. Zenon Rybel, T/3 Hyman Baras, S/Sgt. James W. Mims, M/Sgt. Curtis Packard, T/3 Paul Vance. Seated: 1st Lt. John Miller

1st Lt. John Miller

S/Sgt. James W. Mims

morn and enjoyed that a lot. Thought about you all, of course.

Today our chickens (Paul acquired a tough old rooster) met their doom. Except one hen flew the coop literally. We dressed them (1 rooster-tough--one hen-tough) and put them to boil trying to tender them a bit. We're just getting them out and will try to fry them now. MENU: Salted peanuts, Fried chicken(?), candied comotes, fried comotes (latter courtesy Philippines), canned tomatoes, rice and chicken soup, canned fruit cocktail, visayas (taste like nectarines) crackers, jam, butter, coffee and cigarettes! But we've been cooking all afternoon (it's 4:20) and it's beginning to look like we'll eat the stuff for breakfast!

Am full to the top, now. In fact we're all about to pop. Just like cloverdale picnics. Paul built us a "Field Expedient Sod Buster, Holer one M-3 1944, Philippine Model" which will no doubt soon be in use!

All my love,
James

November 28, 1944
Philippine Is.

Dear Folks,

The island is covered with coconut palms in poor condition now for not having been worked in more than 2 years. This place sends a great deal of copra to the states. I've gotten to like coconut juice very much, the green nuts being quite full. A machete is necessary first to hack off the husk to get to the nut. This is a sort of art. A native with his bolo can do it with about 2 whacks and just skin the nut enough to make a little hole to drink from. The young meat is a delicacy, too, and not as dry as the kind you buy at home. Another good edible part of the palm is the palm heart, which is right in the top of the tree. Shell fragments topple them off sometimes and after chopping the fronds off you can dig out the heart. It tastes a bit like cel-

Master Sergeant Curtis Packard

ery but much more delicate. Since a palm costs about $45.00, and removing the heart kills the tree, it is a rather expensive treat.

Then there are groves of bamboo, ferns, and lots of other greenery. There are many streams, but they are all polluted, and filled with snails which carry liver fluke. So we don't use them. It's also verboten to go barefoot so as to not catch hook worm. Insects are bad, and there are spiders which measure at least 4 inches across which crawl into everything. We're used to it now and it doesn't bother us much anymore.

The clothes the little children wear tickles me. They consist of a shirt which reaches to the general region of the waist. I don't see the logic of it, but they don't seem to mind. The older ones love to wear white, which I've never seen dirty. It's always spotless which is a wonder in this mud. Everyone goes barefoot except a few boys who clomp around in G.I. brogans. And they all hate the Japs extremely. I sent Mother some pictures, so you can get an idea of some of this. For our recreation at night we have done everything from having a spelling bee to discussing politics. All in all we're very lucky, having a good team and are generally comfortable. Except for air raids, it's been quiet.

Well, this won't seem like Christmas, being so warm, but I bet we have turkey. Our cooks would do any restaurant proud, for they are excellent. The best I've seen in the army.

My regards to you all and my love,
James

Nov. 29, 1944

Dear Folks,
Well, the Philippines are quite a place--about hip-deep in mud at present! There's a water buffalo tethered across the street, and various Philippinos meandering about. My, how they like white clothes! It beats me how they can keep them so clean in all this filth, but they are dazzling. Saw one fellow going to church in a brilliant white dinner coat and clean blue pants accompanied by 3 or 4 others clean but bare footed! The people are not undernourished at all but do need clothes. Dado, quite a few of the young'uns need a few ruffles. All they wear is a short shirt!

Now we don't have to do our laundry. For a peso and 50 centaros, the natives will do that. What a relief!

Our cooks here are really excellent. The turkey(!) they fixed for Thanksgiving was a marvel, and they make delicious cakes and pies. There's no call to complain about the food, everything considered.

We are fairly comfortable as long as we keep dry. Sleep in jungle hammocks which have a waterproof top and mosquito netting. They are quite comfortable. It's very hard to get clothes dry but the corresponding coolness from the overcast skies is very refreshing.

When it rains here, it certainly does a good job. Follows Morton's Salts' slogan and really pours. In a typhoon we get the wind, too. One night we were in our tent all blacked out, during one of those. Every time a gust of wind hit, we all had to stop and hold on to the tent! What a night.

I'm trying to learn Tagalog so I can speak with the natives. Many words are Spanish, which should help, and the pronunciation is the same. There's a girl, Maria Murphy (!) by name, who invited me over to teach me! She says she already has 3 others who come over to learn dialect!

All my love,
James

16 Jan. 1945
Philippine Islands

Dear Folks,
Here I go again--still limited by censorship, so I have to try to think of something new to write about a life which is purely routine. It's a mess but here's a noble try.

Well, we are now in a state, best described, I guess, as maintenance of equipment, which means sewing on buttons, dubbing shoes, cleaning weapons, and doing maintenance work on the vehicles. Baras and I went to a place, the name of which figured in the news earlier in this campaign (wouldn't you like to know which?!) to wash some of the accumulated mud and dirt off the jeep. Various Philippine women were washing clothes, beating the daylights out of them with a wooden paddle and smoking nauseating, black cigars, --quite redolent. An odor resembling a cross between a burning pile of cow chips and cabbage. They like them, obviously. But ignoring all obstacles, we doffed the better part of our clothes and went to work on the jeep. After a few hours, I began to wonder why one doesn't see more pottery for when dry, this gumbo is just like cement. We made fair success of our work, though, and returned to our area in time for a bath.

Did I ever tell you about our showers? A far cry from the uncivilized contraption we had in Guinea. Due to a very far-sighted moonlight requisition by certain members of H.2. Co., we are the proud possessors of a machine which manufactures showers. But they are not just "showers." Perish the thought. This wonderful invention spoils us badly by providing a purely civilian luxury--HOT showers! Not like 1917--18, eh Dad? It's really remarkable, but ah! So enjoyable. At least we can really clean up once in a while and enjoy the feeling until we again venture out into the mud.

Love,
James

January 23, 1945
P.I.

Dear Folks,
This is going to be a tough letter to write because there's practically no news here at present; so, I guess I'll have to make this out of whole cloth--

We're very busy though not working too hard. Today we were clearing an area for a baseball diamond, but in this climate, a game like that is plenty strenuous. Yesterday, Sunday, we played some volley-ball and really enjoyed it.

MP on guard at our command post on Leyte

Drove into the town where we were before (we) moved to where we are now and mailed home some clothes and about a carton of cigarettes for you, Dad. Someone sent them to Paul, but the box came open so you'll be that much better off. We dropped in the Red Cross and had some coke, room temperature and made with the usual chlorinated water.

About the only things of souvenir value here are bolos, hats, and sandals. Intend to send something soon, and if the post office will take it, I'll send a ripe coconut this week. Here's how to open them.

Cut the husk like the dotted line, and lop off the top of the husk. Then peel the slices of husk away. It's a hard job. The little ball inside the coconut proper is considered a delicacy here.

Am absolutely fresh out of things to write, so I'll quit.

All my love,
James

January 27, 1945
Philippine Islands

Dear Folks,
Am sorry that all my letters have been delayed, but I try to continue writing every week, and you may be sure that you'll hear any bad news very quickly. So try not to worry when my letters are delayed. It's a policy of the command to provide security for moves by holding mail several days, but it worries me that they don't go through quickly at times.

Due to censorship, there is a blanket rule that no mention of location is permitted, even in the initial invasion. Though the papers announced our location, it was made a policy that we not mention our landing place, for units move from one place to another and it's hard to enforce a rule once broken. Haven't seen the invasion beach since we landed, but may drive around tomorrow and get some pictures for our record. Don't know if I'll get that far or not.

Last week we went on a patrol looking around and I got an idea of this country back from the road. It's rugged going--mud, streams, brush, grass, etc. I was on the point going through a field of cogon grass shoulder high, when I suddenly disappeared from view! Fell in a hole about 3 ½ feet deep--old abandoned foxhole or something. Really felt funny, it happened so quick. Waded a few steams, followed caribou trails, slogged through the inevitable rice paddies, etc. The air corps man who, when asked how field construction was going said, "This is a good island for raising rice," in an exasperated way, was quite right. Perhaps you read that in time.

Another picture of the "Jaro express"!

Luzon still seems to be going very well and I guess we'll soon have to bone up on Chinese. Mallory wrote a letter before they left for that show and said they were very busy. He sent the enclosed Jap invasion money used where he was last stationed.

I'll mail you a mature coconut in a few days, before next week at the latest. It should make good cake.

All my love,
James

Mindoro, 1945

Mindoro, how different from Leyte. The 19th Regiment had invaded the island at San Jose on December 15th with almost no opposition, and the 21st Regiment had invaded far up the coast on the east side at Calapan, also with little opposition. For some reason, our photo team had nothing to do with the planning of this operation. The area around San Jose was a large plain and was quickly turned into five airfields. This gave air support to the invasion of Luzon and control of the sea routes. By the time we arrived, it was secure. I don't recall that we had a single air ride there.

I don't remember anything about our trip from Leyte to Mindoro, or even how we unloaded our landing ship, tank (LST). I do remember coming into the harbor and seeing a P-38 circling high. It began a shallow dive, didn't pull out, and the pilot ejected and floated down to the ocean in his parachute. The plane crashed at sea, and a launch headed out to the rescue. There was no enemy action and we never learned what happened.

We had a comfortable set up at Mindoro. There was a large frame house built up on stilts, the prewar home of the manager of the sugar plantation, which we took over as division headquarters. There was a swimming pool, a baseball diamond, and frequent movies. We set up our pyramidal tents in rows in what had been the garden and dug wide and deep ditches to carry off the rainwater. I don't remember that it ever rained a drop while we were there. It was hot and dry.

We were in the take-off pattern of a bunch of B-25s. Early in the morning, they would take off over us and nearly blow us away! They are a noisy plane and the sound was deafening. They flew lots of missions.

There was a sugar mill made of corrugated metal near us. It reminded me of a West Texas cotton gin and was the only thing that stood up above the trees. One morning we heard a big noise and ran out of the tent to see a P-57 with a 500-point bomb attached stuck in the tower of the mill! We wondered how in the world he managed to hit it. The bomb did not explode and we heard the pilot was not hurt. It did present quite a problem to get the bomb defused and the plane removed.

One Sunday morning about 11:00 o'clock we were in our office tent working on pictures of Lubang, which we were to invade soon, and there was an explosion. We all hit the ground. Then we quickly ran outside just in time to see the remnants of a plane still falling and a pilot in his parachute almost down. The wreckage had hit in a tent area almost adjacent to us. We heard that no one was hurt, but had it been thirty minutes later when everyone came in to get ready for chow, it could have killed many. Again we never found out the cause.

We had elements of our division all over, but no full division activity. The 34th Regiment was in on the invasion of Bataan and on February 16, 1945, of Corregidor. The 503rd Parachute Infantry Regiment made the air drop, staging from Mindoro. We had friends with them, and when they returned, they brought us some captured canned crab and lobster. It was delicious.

Invasion of Mindoro

We were busy working on the invasion of the island of Lubang. We did mapping and discovered some sort of camouflaged installation on top of the mountains in the center of the island, which we found out later was some sort of radar. We could find no defensive areas, and there were in fact none to be found. This was a small engagement involving the First Battalion of the 21st Regiment, which landed on March 1, 1945, and was in control by the end of the week. This led to one of my most memorable experiences.

We had the misfortune of getting stuck on Vienna sausage as our only source of meat for about six weeks, the only relief being caribou-burgers (water buffalo) once or twice. (They were tough!) The Japs had cleaned out all the chickens and other food in our area of Mindoro before we got there, so the natives had nothing to trade. We knew that Lubang was different, but how could we get up there? We found a way!

Lt. Miller made arrangements for me to go with him by PT boat to make some ground photos of the area we had been studying, ostensibly to send back to the States. Off we went, a pair of PT boats at 2 AM on a pitch black morning with no lights. There were still lots of Japs about! I had a half-blanket that I wrapped around me and sat on the deck in front of the cockpit, dozing. We reached the Verde Straits and it got rough, with water splashing all over. I got soaked and then cold—the first time in months! I wondered what my parents would think if they could only see me. I was afraid to move, but I was miserable. So finally I got the courage to inch around the side of the cockpit and to the back, which was a little better. Had I slipped, I'm sure I would have gone straight to the bottom! We landed at Port Tilic after dawn and started walking and hitchhiking up to Lubang Town. My shoes were full of water, but we soon dried out in the heat. We found our buddy who was all set to get us a fried chicken dinner—the real reason we had made the trip! But it was not to be.

Someone spotted us and asked if we had come in on the PT boats. When we said "yes," they told us we were wanted at once for the return. We asked if we had time to eat but were told we did not because they had a couple of Jap prisoners to take back. We were quickly transported by weapons carrier back to Port Tilic and took off for Mindoro. It was about 1:30 in the afternoon and as we were contemplating a D-ration chocolate bar for lunch, the skipper asked if we had eaten. When we told him "no," he told us to go down into the galley and they would fix something. The galley on a PT boat is tiny—a built-in table and benches with a hot plate. There they served us, Vienna sausages! They drew their rations the same place we did.

Top: Mindoro sugar plantation rail car; middle and bottom: Pictures from the trip James Mims and John Miller took to Lubang looking for fried chicken!

February 15, 1945
P.I.

Dear Folks,

I'll start this off saying I'm not where I was, but am where I'm now at, but not where you think I am. It's somewhere else. Now that's probably military info of the most pronounced type, so it'll get censored, but perhaps not!

At last I've something to write, a description of the terrain. "This charming isle of _____, located in the Philippine archipelago, and inhabited by Philippinos, is a veretable gem of ancient culture, dating back years before the Spanish conquest, back when the bolo was an instrument of war, to protect the humble, thatched huts of the natives, unchanged to this day. Covered with lush cogon grass, which houses millions of rats, infamous among mariners of the ages, a tough bamboo, and trees which resemble the cottonwood, or Alamo, also the ombú of Argentina, this isle is truly a sight to see. This lush verdure is also invaluable to the natives, who have only to wrest their legs from the more of the rice fields and retire to this ethereal bower of vegetation and secure in its protection, answer the calls of nature.

Stretching inland from the beach is the small valley, center of agricultural activity. Here the peasants spend their lives in the fields, their large hats sheltering them from the merciless sun, tailing from dawn 'til dark to produce their rice. Here too, is produced a refined sugar which you drop in your tea.

Surrounding the small valley, irrigation by streams, the glory of many dark skinned Isaac Waltons, lie the jagged teeth of the mountains, reaching into the blue their barren crags brown in the distance.

But the island has changed. Where once the bare feet of the natives trod in the worm-infested dust behind their Oriental captors the American machines of war rumble and fly and the liberating soldiers settle happily unto the G.I. routine of tough top sergeants, K.P., and basic training.

We've been working rather hard the last few days. But it's what we're trained for and I enjoy it. It's only when the situation slows that it gets boring. That is war, however. Monotony most of the time with action once in a while.

All my love,
James

Tents set up, at the plantation's garden, on Mindoro

February 26, 1945

Dear Folks,

You wouldn't believe it but the sand is blowing for all the world like a spring day at home! Quite a surprise.

I'm sending a few scenes typical of the Islands, and a few to indicate the type of work which occupies quite a bit of my time. As you see, I'm still holding together pretty well. Naturally I get rather disgusted at times; I never did like to be told what to do. Am also enclosing some guerrilla money which was used here in the Islands when the Japs were around. I wouldn't doubt but that it might be valuable some time.

I see by the news that the 24th is really getting around! We've been busy lately in fixing our tents, deep ditches, racks over our cots, etc. and now have a very livable place. The wind keeps blowing just like home and it's very dry. Rain starts in another month I think.

Did I tell you about the sensitive plant which grows here? It has tiny leaves like those on heel-burrs, and closes up when touched. Lt. Rybel sneaked up on one today with a little notebook and snapped it closed on a leave before it knew what happened! I'll try the same thing and send you a stem!

I started to mail you that coconut, but it had to be censored! Then we got entangled in moving and I didn't get it mailed. There aren't as many here, but one of these days I'll send you one.

All my love,
James

March 12, 1945

Trip to Lubang

Dear Folks,

Time to write another letter, but I am positively out of news completely!

This week we're doing a little training in terrain appreciations. That consist of personally looking over various hills and rocks and isn't very interesting. Went to one of the saw mills this morning.

Unfortunately the infant firm of Mobray and Mims is in dire need. The eldest member of the firm has joined the 41st. Perhaps, however, it is for the best. He and Jerry can cover the 41st and I can handle the 24th end of it. So I'll just describe our progress as "expansion."

The main event in H.Q. these days is the baseball league now in effect. Some of the games are very good.

Tents at Mindoro

We had a change in the weather Sunday in the way of a shower. It cooled things off a lot and settled to dust. There's promise of more, for it's cloudy tonight. Unfortunately our tent leaks in a few places.

I read one of the most accurate descriptions of the war the other day, containing all those things we can't write. It's an article in an old *Life* titled "Our Army in Western Europe." It's very good, giving proper credit and unprejudiced criticism.

Love,
James

Mindanao, 1945

Our next assignment was working on the invasion of Mindanao. The Japs had anticipated that our first invasion of the Philippines would come in Davao Gulf, so there were multiple defensive positions in depth. However, they had not anticipated that we would come in the back door! Our landing was to be at Parang and Cotobato on the west coast across the bay from Zamboanga, which had already been taken by the 41st Division. We mapped the landing area from our photos but found no entrenchments. We left Mindoro on another Friday 13th, this one in April 1945. Our trip by landing ship, tank (LST) was almost like a cruise. The most noteworthy thing I remember was getting the news that President Franklin Roosevelt had died, and that Vice President Harry Truman was now president.

Packer and Miller made the landing and the rest of us came in a couple of days later. Miller was right near Colonel Bill Verbeck, the regimental commander, when he got shot by a sniper. This is Moro country. We had been carefully instructed to leave these people strictly alone, and one look at them convinced us this was the wise thing to do. They were a fierce and mean-looking bunch, but we did not stay in their area for long. Jap resistance was light and sporadic, and we took off across the island for the Davao side, covering the more than one hundred miles in about two weeks. We were on the so-called National Highway, a narrow dusty gravel road running from coast to coast. In the middle of the island, the Sayre Highway branched off north and was taken by the 31st Division, which was following us. The country was cut by multiple streams and rivers with all the bridges blown either by our retreating troops back in 1941 or lately by the Japs. High mountains, including the extinct volcano Mt. Apo, dominated the center of the island, and jungle covered a large area, which our maps showed simply as "unexplored." It was another extremely spooky place, like Leyte.

Our position was highly exposed. We were stretched out on a road forty-feet wide and more than one hundred miles long! We did have air cover from Zamboanga and little harassment from Jap planes by this time, but there were frequent ambushes by Jap patrols. At night we put out perimeter guards, and most everyone dug in. One night, a signal corpsman bunked in with us. He strung a hammock between some trucks, along with two other fellows, one of whom was Don Twining. During the night, Don who suffered from asthma, could not sleep so he unzipped his hammock and leaned over to put on his shoes. He accidentally bumped the signal corpsman, who promptly screamed and came out of his hammock waving a machete! To which Don calmly said, "Shut up, you fool!" But this woke everyone. I had dug a hole and put my hammock down in it, leaving my rifle leaning against a palm tree, totally out of reach. And I did not dare try to move because all you could hear was people jacking shells into the chambers of their weapons! Then a voice, "It's alright! It's one of our men." So we all relaxed and went back to a fitful sleep. The next morning the signalman did not even wait for breakfast!

Camouflaged boat

We went through beautiful country. General Woodruff really made the division move by whatever method was available, including using landing craft! He moved part of the 34th Regiment up the Mindanao River that way, kept the enemy off balance, and took lots of ground quickly. The road ran across the island until it reached Davao Gulf, where it turned north up the coast to Davao City. One day our convoy was moving right along when we began to pass soldiers walking on both sides of the road, who shouted out asking who we were. When we told them we were division headquarters, they laughingly told us they were the point of advance! We were just about to take their place, so we quickly stopped and regrouped! That day we found warm rice on tables in the huts in a small village left by the just departed Japs!

Near the turn northward and up the coast, we began to encounter bombs that had been buried nose up along the side of the road. These acted like landmines; if they were run over, they would detonate. The Japs also had some they set off manually with long wires or cords. We drove extremely carefully in this area and some of our forward troops had had real trouble with this tactic.

We moved on up the coast to a place called Talomo and set up our command post there. It was a beautiful spot right on the Gulf of Davao in a palm grove with good sandy soil, not mud as on Leyte, and only a few miles south of Davao City, which we had not as yet captured. The terrain sloped gently upward from the Gulf twenty or thirty miles to Mt. Apo, an extinct volcano, which dominated the western skyline. This area was covered with jungle and abaca or hemp plantations that had not been tended in months offering perfect concealment. The roads surrounding the fields were grown up in under-brush and each was a defile. The Japs had pulled back into this area and there were lots of them! It was tailor made for ambushes, which were frequent and deadly. We were in easy artillery range and one day we did have a few rounds come over and land in the bay. They would only fire a few rounds at a time because as soon as we could locate a gun, our artillery would take them out. One day a Major Morgan with division artillery went up in the spotter plane to try to find a Jap gun that was giving us trouble and got shot at a good bit by some enemy anti-aircraft. He came back to our tent to try to locate the target on our photos and was telling us about his experience. He said “They just kept shooting at us and I kept getting nervouser and nervouser!” Considering how vulnerable a cub plane is, that was real easy to understand!

One day a prisoner was brought in. He claimed to be with an aircraft repair unit that our Order of Battle people showed to be in China, not Mindanao. Careful questioning solved the mystery. His unit had shipped out and somehow left him behind, so he had just been going from one unit to another doing the best he could. Finally they gave him a rifle, put him in a foxhole, and told him to die for the Emperor. Either bombing or artillery had covered him up, and our troops had dug him out and captured him. Even the Japs had snafus, too!

There were many Japs and Jap sympathizers in the Davao City area. There was a tent field hospital south of Talomo, and one of our counterintelligence men went there to interrogate a wounded Filipino. Several days later he and some others were ambushed at a bridge near the hospital, and he got shot through the tail! Most of the Japs were killed, but the Filipino who had guided the Jap patrol was wounded, captured, and carried to the hospital where the counterintelligence man was also taken. There they met, and the counterintelligence man became livid. This was the same Filipino he had so recently interrogated! The hospital had released him, he had gone back to the hills to rejoin the Japs, and had promptly guided another patrol! The American really chewed him out for taking our free medical attention, and then leading the patrol that shot him in the rear! He was one mad soldier!

The 41st Division had taken Zamboanga several weeks before our division landed at Cotobato, and the Marines had set up an air field. There was a small dirt strip near Talomo called Libby Drome, and they would fly in there and come to us to get targets. Once we identified what we thought was some sort of Jap supply and dump and command post. We showed the photos to the pilots, who took off, but soon returned unable to find the site. We picked out a field that was shaped like a hand pointing directly toward the target. They took off again, quickly found the field and then the target. As we lazily swam in Davao Gulf in front of our command post, we watched as they dive bombed and strafed! Later we heard that we had been right, and that the Japs lost some high-ranking officers in that air attack.

I had another spooky experience here. Our command post was on a slightly raised area in a palm grove with the Gulf on one side and a swamp on the opposite. I was on the perimeter guard in a foxhole with another soldier one night on the swamp side. I had an M-1, and for safety's sake, I had not put a bullet into the chamber but had only slid the bolt partially in and put on the safety. That means that I would have to hit the bolt handle to seat the bullet before I could fire, which would make a noise. It was pitch black and we were alert for the slightest sound. Suddenly there was a terrible crashing sound! But it was only a dead palm frond falling from a tree. We settled back down. And then much later, we heard a sound coming from the swamp—a squish! And in a while, another! And after another short interval, another! It sounded like someone trying to walk silently through the muck of the swamp. We had a whispered conference and decided that when the sound got a little closer, my buddy would fire a couple of the rounds, I would slam the bullet into the chamber of my gun, try to see something by the muzzle blast, and shoot if I could find the target. But we didn't take into account the fellows in the hole next to us. They had also heard the sounds and suddenly fired a couple of shots! We saw nothing by the light of their muzzle blasts. All was absolutely quiet for a long time. And then, squish, and after a long interval, another squish, and finally another, and another, all going away. We never knew who had been out there that night, but they must have been as frightened as we were.

We continued our work because the division was still heavily engaged. We were getting photos regularly and studied them very hard. On one set, we identified what we believed to be a cave in a bluff on a river, which was likely a Jap storage depot. It was fairly near and supposedly out of the main combat area, so our jeep driver, Hargens, together with the fellow who had been on my landing craft at Leyte, Don Twining, and others took our jeep to go see, looking for souvenirs. That was a mistake! A Jap sniper took a shot at them, the bullet went through the bar supporting the jeep top, and through Don's mouth, knocking out some teeth. Pieces of metal also hit Hargens in the arm. Don was in the hospital and died not longer after the division arrived in Japan for occupation duty, supposedly from the effects of the antibiotics.

Landing craft infantry vessel

Aerial photos of camouflaged Japanese barracks, Mindanao

April 1945
Board Ship

Dear Folks,

This stationery came just before we left and I like it a lot. There is only one mistake. I'm not in H2. Cf. but in Division Headquarters. Here's the set up. There is a maj. general commanding, a brigade general 2nd in command and the staff which consists of G-1, 2, 3, and 4--all Lt. Colonels. There are several officers and enlisted men in each section. That Div. H.2. HQ. Co. is a company which has charge of the motor pool, the defense platoon, etc. Since I've worked with G-2, I'm in Div. H.2.

We can now write about Leyte, though no doubt you suspected that I was there! We landed near Palo and were about a mile from the town the second night when 70 or 80 Japs came in there and raised the devil. Then we went on up to Alongalong, Jaro, Carigara, Culasion point, and then back to Jaro. Remember the picture of the Caribou cart. That was what we called the Jaro-Carigara bus line. We used to wash the jeep in the River of Jaro. I did go to Jackobon once just before we left the island, but it's not much. We spent Christmas Eve at Culasion Pt. which is about a mile or so from Luriou and breakneck ridge where we had such a tough fight.

This is the nicest ocean trip I've ever had. You can't imagine just how dark blue the water is. The sky is practically clear of clouds, the all tropical sun is beating down, and the sea is glassy. The soft swish of foam from the progression of the ship is quite soothing. We saw a couple of sharks fins and a few flying fish. Oh yes. When we left Leyte we saw a couple of whales I don't think I told you about.

On this trip on of the most interesting things I've seen happened, reminding me of Milne Bay. While stopped in a port, we saw the natives come out to the boats in their outrigger canoes. They were trading chickens and what have you. But the interesting thing was to see them dive for money like the Fiji islanders. Quite romantic, isn't it?

We made our landing with no difficulty and joined Packard and Lt. Miller. You didn't remember Packard, you wrote, so I'll refer you to my New Guinea series, if you have them. We were in a very cool coconut grove and the weather was agreeable.

We made quite a jump and the ride was very interesting. It was cool at the start and we rode on the truck fenders. The scenery was magnificent and we saw all kinds of vegetation. Avocados, breadfruit, cocoa, bananas, limes, papayas, and corn. Looks like we'll have pretty good chow. Ate some breadfruit which tastes a little like cantaloupe. Eventually the sun got pretty high and it was the hottest I can remember! The people here are very friendly and of higher quality than those of Leyte.

I had a remarkable experience last night. Had my hammock tied at one end to a coconut tree and the other end tied to a pole in a nipa house. Packard, unfortunately, was also tied to the same pole. We just got to sleep when--Blam--the whole house collapsed on top of me! First time I ever had a house fall on me so literally. So far this is a much more interesting spot than Leyte and we like it better, except for the tremendous heat. Will write more when I can.

All my love,
James

May 2, 1945
Philippine Islands

Dear Folks,
Well, by now we are well on our way. This is to me much different than Leyte, and I believe I'll enjoy each new invasion less instead of more. We had a long, hot, dusty ride, but, the scenery here far exceeds anything I've seen yet. There are all kinds of vegetation. Everything seems to grow here, including mosquitos big enough to knock a person down! We've had bananas, papayas, avocados, and mangoes to eat. Also pineapples. We picked our avocados and let them ripen. Very good they are.

It is really hot these days. We've been riding on the front fender of the truck, and the dust and the heat make a very unpleasant combination. I'm afraid to bathe in the streams for they are all polluted, so we have to confine ourselves to a spit bath from a helmet. When I get to Frisco I'm going to get a hotel room, eat breakfast in bed, take a good bath, put on clean clothes, shoot the works in the barber shop, and head for a drug store, ice cream and cold milk. But I'm afraid that will be a long time yet.

Being constantly on the move, I haven't kept up too well on the news, but it seems that Germany must quit any day. I hope Japan will soon do the same, for they haven't a chance, but they are peculiar people and very good fighters.

I can't think of another thing to write. Hope you enjoyed your trip to Denton. And a happy Mother's Day.

All my love,
James

May 9, 1945
P.I.

Dear Folks,
Well today marks the passing of another week or two. Of course the big news is the German surrender. It has had such a strange effect. No one cheers or slaps you on the back. Previously every night we would all gather around the recon vehicle to hear the news. Now it's over (the German Mess.) and there isn't too much interest. Last night was the first time the Philippine Hour has broadcast the Pacific news first. We used to listen to that newscast back in Guinea and Leyte. The general attitude is "Why don't the Japs give up? They are really in for it now. Boy, I can hardly wait to see some of that European stuff over here!" But the artillery just keeps on pounding. I jump every time they fire! But it's nice to hear those shells carump on the Nips.

Our troops advancing on Mindanao

You asked me to tell you something of the fellows here. There is one boy, a draftsman in G-2, by name Fred Goettinger, who is quite a card. About my age, he is from New York. His favorite pastime is comparing New York with Hollywood wherein the Californian metropolis usually comes out the small end. This is all for the benefit of Floyd Flom, from Hollywood. Floyd's friends, Bob (Taylor). Judy (Farlow(?)) etc., are usually maligned until Flom gets furious. Fred is quite a boy. I usually come in for my share, too, being the only Texas boy in the section.

This is an odd sort of war over here. I shouldn't write this because I'll lose all my sympathy! The other day while taking a swim in the blue Pacific we watched planes bomb and strafe Japs a very short distance away. Imagine! There are

Camp Pikit

plenty of the boys whose luck isn't quite that good, however.

All my love,
James

May 24, 1945
Philippine Islands

My dear Mother and Sister

I have just come from the Red Cross where I had the message of Dad's passing away. I can't realize it as yet; it seems so unreal and far away. Mr. Dyson, the Red Cross field director told me that you wished and needed me at home. I can't offer much hope as it is hard for a man to be released over here, especially when they have only been over a short time. I'll see exactly what the situation is and write again tomorrow and will try to make it.

I didn't know of Dad's even being sick. The telegram gave no particulars and only mentioned the death. The thing that makes it so strange is that I dreamed it last night.

I don't yet know how to accept it. How I would love to come home to enjoy his kidding and laugh and all that was my father, but how thankful I am that we had so many years of fun together. Dad never lacked for lots of friends so I know that I need not worry for your being cared for until I can again return home. It's a time of universal pain and suffering and perhaps it is only right that we should feel our share.

I can't write anymore. I'm in good shape and the campaign is progressing with more success each day. We all pray that very soon this thing will be over.

All my love Mother and Sister. May God help us all--
James

Parang, Mindanao

25 May 1945

Dear Mother and Sister,

I have put in my application for an emergency furlough, but it is certain that it will be at least 3 weeks before I will get any answer to the request. There is, unfortunately, little that I can do personally to expedite matters. Will just have to hope and pray. I'm worried very much and hope that letters will come very soon. I presume that Cousin Joe is handling what legal matters are pressing and I know that we have many friends to do all they can.

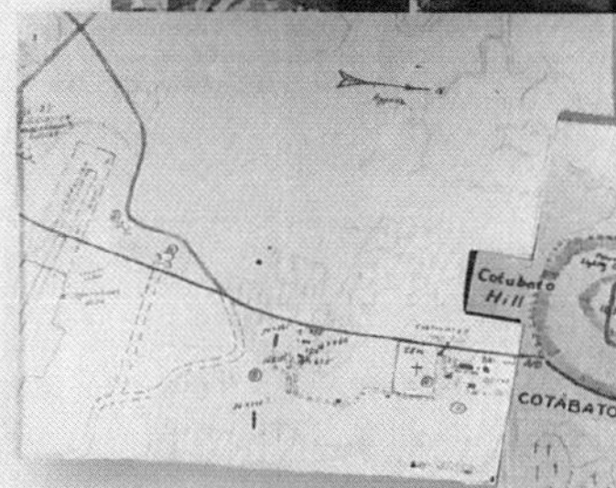

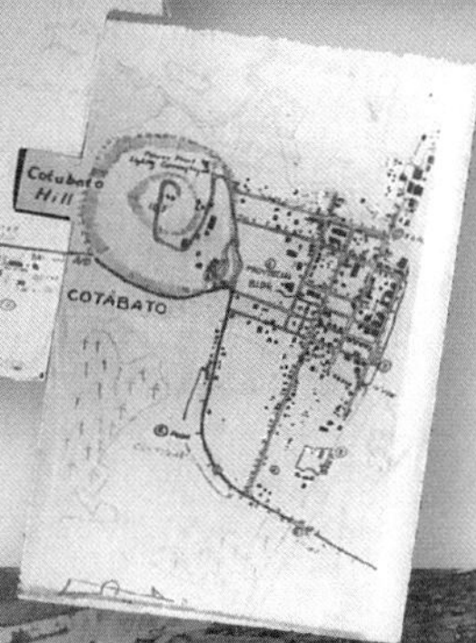

Cotabato, Mindanao—Moro Country

I've submitted request for a class B dependency allotment, stating that you are 60% dependent upon me for support. This will be checked by the war department representatives who will determine the correct amount. I will send my copy to Cousin Joe for his information. I'll explain more fully to him. I am also sending him a copy of my request for furlough so that he will be cognizant of my situation in case he should need to be.

Top and middle: West side of Mindanao; bottom: highway across Mindanao

I feel utterly helpless since at present I know nothing except the bare facts of the telegram which stated that "Dad was gone and my presence was needed for business purposes." It will be necessary to prove through the Red Cross that the family will lose financially if I do not get home. I trust that you and Sister will be able to manage without undue money troubles until such time as I can get some information or sent home.

I feel very incapable to step in Daddy's shoes but will do everything that I can, which is very little, I fear. It's infuriating to be here so far away for I know you need me very much.

Please take care of yourself, Mother and let me know as soon as possible what you wish to do. If only mail would come! I might as well be on Mars. I feel like I'm a million, million miles away.

I love you with all my heart.
James

May 27, 1945
Philippine Islands

Dearest Mother and Sister,
As far as I am able to see, I've done everything that I can do here. I'm sending in another envelope the copies of a power of attorney document I have made out, giving you my power of attorney. If this is not satisfactory, let me know as soon as you can and I'll follow whatever suggestion you make.

My request for furlough has gone in, but to be frank, I have next to no hope of it being granted. Since we are in action, it doesn't seem promising, but there is a bare chance. I wrote Cousin Joe more completely about it, and know he will do whatever is possible there. Keep your fingers crossed.

From what I know of the business situation at home, there is more than we can handle; I suppose, then, we will stand to lose financially now that Dad has gone. I don't

Top: Bulldozer being unloaded from landing craft during invasion; middle: Curtis Packard and others at Parang; bottom: The "Moros."

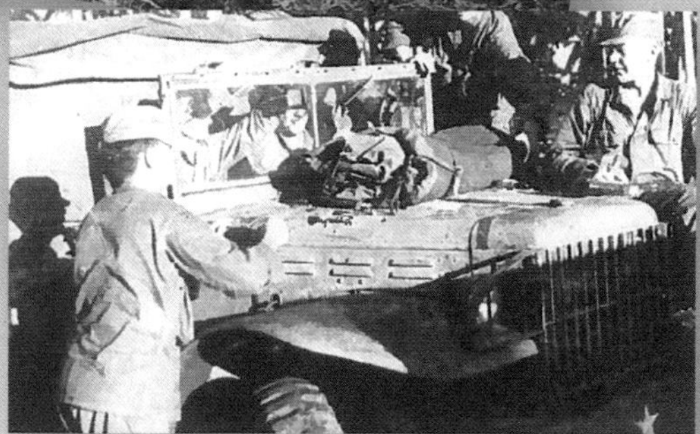

Top: Damage in the Parang area after invasion; middle: dead Japanese after invasion; bottom: James Mims, Zenon Rybel, and others in the truck that carried them on the fenders 150 miles across the island.

know whether you will want to sell the car, stay home or go to Tyler for a while or what. I'm very anxious to know if Sister will be able to stay in school or not. Try to tell me as much of what you plan as possible. Of course I know you will as soon as I get mail, but it takes so long.

The Lt. gave me the day off, the first since we landed in April. We've worked steadily everyday, but have not had too much night work. I really feel that we've done a great deal for the operation, especially when compared with Leyte.

I'm anxiously awaiting more news.

I love you very much,
James

May 31, 1945
Philippine Islands

Dear Mom and Sister,

I'm still very anxious to get a letter from you and expect one tomorrow or the next day. I had a letter today from Sue Miles dated the 17th, which was very nice. She mentioned that Uncle Basil, too, is gone, which was an additional shock. I guess from that it must have been an accident. Honestly I've never felt so far away and helpless. It seems as though I'm hanging by a thread in space.

My application for furlough has gone in and hasn't been returned as yet. I'm hoping, though.

I hope you are feeling well, Mother. Naturally I worry about you and Sister very much, even when I know there are many friends who will help in every way they can.

Our work has slowed a little in the last few days, but there's still plenty to keep us busy. Yesterday Lt. Miller and Glen Hargens, our new man on the team, acquired a Jap auxiliary fuel tank for an airplane. We finally got a hole in the top and took it to the water point. Hargens filled it only about half-full but we couldn't carry it. Finally, however, we got it installed on a rack, so we have running water. Lt. Miller affixed a salvaged faucet to one end.

All my love to you both,
James

Our troops advance.

Jack Waltz, OB Team, James Mims, PI Team, and another colleague taken in Mindanao

Order of the Pick and Shovel

5 June, 1945

Dearest Folks,
I've still had no letters from you for reasons which I've explained before. But I did get a letter from Cousin Joe (May 17) and at least know the details of the death.

I've written Cousin Joe to give him more detail about my application for furlough. It has been approved by Division and has gone on to Corps. Perhaps they will give it their O.K., too.

We had fresh meat today for dinner and it was really good. Spam and bully beef can really kill an appetite after awhile. Glen Hargens and Paul went out today and came back with some nice fresh bananas which were very good.

I believe that this is the nicest CP site we've had. It's comparatively cool and the usual rains soak in quickly since the soil is sandy. That's certainly better than any spot in Leyte, which was always knee deep in mud.

I can mention now that the dusty place where we were is Mindoro Island. The little island, Lubang Island. If you have a map of the Philippines you can probably find them alright. Would like to have visited Manila and perhaps will have a chance some day.

The Japs continue to resist as stubbornly as is customary with them. But where we can get replacements of everything, they can't. That puts them in the same place we were when they invaded the Philippines some few months ago. It's really poetic justice.

Top: General Arthur Stillwell and group; middle: Australian Dignitary and Our Commander, General Woodruff, among others; bottom: "parafrag" bombs dropped by U.S. planes

This life is very boring. Where in Europe it was possible to get passes to various cities, there's no place to go here if one gets a pass. There's nothing to do except play cards or read. Glad I'm just bored and not scared all the time like the fellows up front. There's lots of difference between this and Leyte. We've only seen one airborne Jap plane since we landed.

Keep your fingers crossed on my furlough--

All my love,
James

June 9, 1945

Dear Folks,
I still have had no mail and I'm beginning to get good and mad. These pinheads are so lazy and have to follow so many details of an order that they lose sight of the deed for the doing. You used to laugh at me, wanting to be a garbage collector. Well, even that has advantages over army life!

I've had no further word about a furlough. It has passed division, I know, and has gone to corps for their O.K.

Mother, I know you and Sister must be very lonely these days and it makes me furious, the way they don't get our mail here. However, we've had fresh meat several times recently--about 6 times in 4 months. Guess we have to look after the "poor" European peoples first.

There's nothing in the world to write. I'm O.K. with nothing ailing me except wanting to get home!

All my love,
James

Top: Landing craft full of soldiers on the Mindanao River; bottom: little Town on the East Coast of Mindanao

General Joe "Vinegar Joe" Stillwell and party;

Mindanao Bridge destroyed by retreating American troops in 1942

James Mims, Zenon Rybel, and Paul Vance still on Mindanao!

On the night of May 23, 1945, I decided to sleep in the back of our truck. It had the usual canvas cover, so I was out of the weather and there was some protection from the mosquitos. I dreamt that I could see Mother and Sister together, crying uncontrollably. There was no context to the dream, only the one scene, but it was so intense that it woke me up! I soon went back to sleep.

About 9:00 the next morning I had a call to go over to the Red Cross tent. Some of the fellows suggested that they might be planning an amateur hour and wanted me to act as emcee as I had done on the ship coming overseas, but I was doubtful. When I came into the Red Cross tent, the Field Director, Mr. Dyson, asked me how long it had been since I had heard from home. I didn't answer but asked him "Did my father die?" He asked again how long it had been since I had a letter from home, and if my father had been ill, so again I asked "Did my father die?" He then told me that he had received a cable that Dad had died on May 15. There were no details and no information about the cause of death.

I made application for a furlough and worried and wondered what could have happened. At home, Daddy's close friend, Fred Wemple who was active in politics was working with Congressman Ewing Thomason and Senator Tom Connally. Cousin Percy Mims, a Lt. Colonel and Adjutant at Bolling Field in Washington, D.C., was contacting officers he knew at the Pentagon. Other friends were writing letters to the Red Cross, all trying to help me get the furlough. I could only wait.

The first word I received only deepened the mystery. I got a letter on May 31 from Dorothy Sue Miles expressing sympathy not only about Dad, but also about Uncle Basil! I was shocked and could only assume there had been a car wreck. Finally, on about June 5, I got a letter from cousin Joe Mims telling me the details. Dad had suffered a heart attack on the morning of May 15 and died that afternoon about 5:00. When Joe went to tell Uncle Basil, he could not find him. Finally Joe climbed up on a saw horse, looked in the kitchen window, and saw Uncle Basil on the floor. They broke in and found him dead, also from a heart attack! Neither ever knew of the death of the other.

My part in the war was rapidly winding down. I did get my furlough and left Mindanao at the end of June. Finally, it was time for me to leave Mindanao for home! My orders called for me to fly—a real break. There was a small dirt airfield near us called Libby Drome. We would have it one day, the Japs the next, and we shared it on the third! I was to catch a C-45 ATC plane there, but when we got to the field, there was a lieutenant in an AT 6 ready to take off for Leyte, who offered me a ride. Rather than wait, I got in the rear cockpit. I could not stow my duffle bag behind the seat, but had to hold it in my lap to keep the plane in trim. He fastened me in with the crash harness and parachute harness, told me not to get into the pedals with my feet, or the throttle with my arm, and we took off, buzzed the field, and headed north. If anything had happened, I could never have gotten out! After several uncomfortable hours, we sighted Leyte. How it had changed! The harbor was full of ships, and the beaches were covered with all kinds of supplies and people. Tacloban Airfield was fully operational, and we landed there. I then caught a plane on to Manila.

I found that I had a three-day wait for my priority to come up to fly out, so that night I bunked in with the XI Corps Photo Interpretation Team, who were set up in a shoe factory downtown. The next day I hitch hiked up to San Fernando, the location of 6th Army Headquarters, to see the two Photo Interpretation Teams there. They were working on plans for the invasion of Japan. A November date had been set, and I looked at all the photos of the area where the 24th was to go in! It reminded me of the pictures we had studied back in the States of the Normandy invasion area with short beaches and steep cliffs. It was frightening to anticipate. And if anyone had known that I had that information, I would not have been permitted to come home at all! Needless to say, I never mentioned this to anyone. The teams were excited because that morning one of their members, Master Sergeant Cheesler from Cleveland in studying the latest serial photos had discovered several camouflaged warships, remnants of the Jap navy! This was a tremendous piece of intelligence and demonstrated the value of our teams to the war efforts. One of the team members drove me back to Manila in his jeep. Jap patriots were often raiding this road, smashing whoever came along, so we didn't terry. Fortunately, we had no trouble. The next day, I left the Philippines.

I was on my way! We left Clark Field in a C-54 and as we reached our cruising altitude, I was cold for the first time in a long while. It was great! The planes we used had bucket seats along the sides, there was nothing to see but clouds and ocean, and little to do but sleep. On one leg of the flight, a nurse, two officers, and I sat on the floor and played bridge. We landed at Saipan, Johnson Island, and then Hickham Field in Honolulu. Bullet marks were still evident from the Pearl Harbor attack. There we had fresh milk, cold Coca Cola, and fresh lettuce and tomatoes. Then on to the United States—a 13-hour flight ending at Hamilton Field, California, about 3:00 AM. We were taken to the mess hall where we each got a quart of fresh milk, a big lettuce and tomato salad, and all the fresh eggs we wanted. What a feast! Then it was time to get cleaned up and see about getting on home. Hooray!!

After going to a barber shop, where I got one of everything they had(!), I went by train to Los Angeles to see Tom Jones's parents (and sister, Sue!). I borrowed a field jacket Tom had left there, because I was cold, even if it was July. My blood was thin from a year in the tropics, and I didn't get warm until the train got to the middle of Arizona. My skin was quite yellow from taking atabrine, an artificial quinine we took daily to ward off the effects of malaria. A month at home passed quickly. I managed a trip to Tyler to see everyone there, went to San Antonio to the 8th Service Command to put in an application for an emergency discharge, enjoyed home cooking and the pleasure of civilian life, and tried to visit everyone. After living outside for a year, sleeping inside in a soft bed and driving a car with a top on it was confining. It felt like being in a box. Too soon it was time to return to Camp Stoneman and back overseas to participate in the invasion of Japan, which I knew was coming soon. I was apprehensive.

Camps Ritchie and Lee, 1945

I reported in to Stoneman and waited for orders to ship out again. One day they brought in 2000 replacements, none older than eighteen years of age, with several young master sergeants in charge. They looked like a bunch of Boy Scouts to me. It was strange to contemplate my own perspective. I was now an "old soldier," but at the same time I realized that I was only four years older than they were. It was a sad thing to know what was about to happen to them. They were so young, green, and vulnerable. Fortunately within just a few days, we dropped the first atom bomb, followed soon by another. Perhaps the Japs would have surrendered anyway, but I believe that this act saved the lives of thousands, perhaps including many of these young soldiers, and mine as well. Had we been required to carry out the invasion of Japan, the loss of life would have been massive. Two days before I was to ship out, my orders were changed. I was soon on my way across the United States and back to Camp Ritchie, Maryland, where I arrived the night of August 14, the date the Japs officially announced their surrender. And I couldn't get a pass to leave camp to celebrate! No matter. It was over! Now the questions was "When do I get to go home?"

I had little to do at Ritchie except wait. Then I got an interesting job, that of Interoffice Paper Passer! The various units in Europe wrote critiques of the different specialty teams that Camp Ritchie had supplied. There were two officers charged with summarizing and correlating these, and they had two clerks to type up the reports. The five of us were assigned a small office and I sat in the middle. As reports were typed, they were given to me to proofread and to hand to the lieutenant, who gave them to the captain. New material or corrections went the other direction and were handed to me to hand to the typists. Some job, but lots better than KP! It was interesting to read all the different outfits in Europe, especially because I knew many of the people on the teams. Then one day I got orders to the Quartermast Corps! But this was just a preliminary to getting my discharge.

At Camp Lee, I was assigned to a company composed of casuals. There were soldiers from everywhere, some from places I had never heard of. Our captain had been in India. There he and his jeep driver saw some Indian signal corpsmen one day practicing with semaphores on the hills around them. To their shock and dismay they discovered that these were not signalmen. Rather, they were guards trying to warn them to get out of the mortar range they had just entered! Too late, as it turned out. His jeep was destroyed and both he and the driver were wounded. He was invalided back to the States and sent to Camp Lee for discharge. It was a matter he really did not care to discuss! They put us at the back of the base pretty well out of sight, and the captain told us that if we would keep a low profile and stay out of trouble, he would try to keep us from having to do details because he, too, was anxious to get out of service and go home. This suited all of us just fine, so we were only too happy to cooperate.

I met a fellow named Keith Warner. He had been with the 103rd Division as a BAR man, got knocked down by the blast from a German 88 shell and wrenched his knee. After a short stay in the hospital, he returned to duty, only to have the same thing happen again, so they sent him home for medical discharge. He, his wife, and two kids lived in Urbana, Illinois. Rationing was still in effect, but because soldiers were being given preference. Keith wanted to go home to get his car so that when he was discharged, he could get some new tires. He and I got a three-day weekend pass and hitchhiked to Urbana. What a wild trip, through the backwoods of West Virginia at night, getting rides of every kind imaginable through Ohio, Indiana, and finally Illinois. We did everything but ride a freight! And then had four flats coming back; Keith did get his tires.

August 3, 1945

Dear Mother and Sister,

Well, this is a letter I'd hoped I wouldn't have to write. It seems the Army just can't get along without me so I'll have to add a few more gold bars to my sleeve and a few more stars to my ribbons.

The lieutenant in personnel section was very nice and said my papers were very well gotten together, so at least we did everything possible. The service command here delegates discharge power to this camp, and they turned down my request because I cannot show that destitution exists at home. So it looks like we'll just have to accept it and make the most of the situation. As I told you when I was home, I have a much better situation than most and must be thankful that you will be able to get along comfortably, at least. Too, I've had a nice rest away from army life for awhile. I have to admit that I'm very blue for I know how bad you need me and what I have to go back to. Now begins the inevitable waiting to get started. I know that you will be very brave and do the best you can. I, too, can prepare for the day we all get home again by studying the business through correspondence courses the army offers. Too, I'll have the satisfaction of knowing I've done my job in the Army until they decide my job is no longer needed.

The last few days the realization that Dad is gone has finally soaked in, and I miss him so much. So many things come to me that I would like to ask his advice about or talk to him about. Seems that Dad always had to work so hard that we never did get to spend much time together. But he left a pattern for life and an example that I can never equal. I don't know what I have ever done to deserve such a father. So few boys can boast of parents like mine. I pray that my resolve to follow the examples he gave never, never weaken and that I can lead a life that will make you and him proud of me.

Mom, did you ever have one of these spells where you sit and think and little things just sort of fall in place; things that don't mean much by themselves, but together make a picture. Perhaps it's a part of growing up. On the train it happened to me--thinking of you and Dad and Sister, of all our friends, the good things people do, church, civic accomplishments--I guess it's sort of forming a philosophy. I don't know how to write it all down exactly, but it sort of makes things fall into their proper places of value and made me feel very good.

Write me at my overseas address and I'll phone as often as I can.

All my love,
James

General Irving, Commander of the 24th Division, and relieved of Command on Leyte

P.S. I feel much better after writing this. It seems so odd the way my life falls into some sort of pattern. All my army life seems to have some reason behind it, the way I didn't get into artillery though I wanted that so badly, A.S.T.P. instead of O.C.S., picked out of a hat for Ritchie instead of the 78th Division with the most of the Boston group. I wonder why my discharge was not granted, but that, too, must fit somewhere in the Bigger Scheme.

August 15th, 1945
Camp Ritchie, Md

Dear Mom and Sister,

Two days before I was to get on a boat, Stoneman got a wire and I've been reassigned to Camp Ritchie. I got into Baltimore Monday and hitch-hiked to Washington. Margaret and

Staff Sergeant James W. Mims

the boys are in Texas, but Cousin Percy and I had a nice little visit. He told me that Uncle Joe was quite sick and had to go to the hospital as I guess you know.

Percy told me that if my discharge request had gone to Washington, it would have been granted. He advised me to re-submit it, and I'll write you in a week or so what to do about it.

I hitch-hiked back to Baltimore and got within about 5 miles of Ritchie (on the train) when the surrender was announced. So it seems that destiny has me again. If I hadn't been reassigned, I would have been out on the Pacific now. Surely there will be a better chance of a discharge now, especially since I am on this side of the water.

Ritchie is dead, for everyone is on a 2 day holiday and I don't know what they will do with me.

The trip was by Pullman but very boring. I guess I'm tired of traveling.

Try as I might, I can't find anything else to write down. My goodness! Co. K. Camp Ritchie, Md.

Love,
James

September 2, 1945

Dear Mom and Sis--
I got my letter from you, Sis, and also one from you, Mother--I can't figure out what's happened to the time, August gone and September here already. It doesn't seem possible.

Here is what must be done on my discharge now. The letter will have to be retyped in triplicate and with no errors exactly as before with these changes.

The copy of the first letter should be at the office somewhere for use as a pattern. Sister, perhaps you can do the typing on it. And instead of triplicate make it in quadruplicate. The affidavits and the original letter I sent in should come back from Cal. Soon because I wrote asking them to be sent to 592 Midland. But don't count on them. Wait about 10 days and if they don't come, try to get the same people, or others, to do them again, original and 3 copies. Send all of it to me when you have it ready. I'll phone next weekend sometime and see if there are any questions.

I have K.P. again tomorrow and have not been doing anything in the least important since I got here. We had a conducted tour of Gettysburg Battlefield last week which was very interesting. Hope we can all come up here sometime. It's truly beautiful country.

A number of the boys in the company have shipped out for more specialized training before going overseas, so there aren't many of us left. Don't know yet if they have any important assignment for me, but I guess I'll find out if and when they do.

Nothing to write except it's very dull and monotonous here.

Hope you are feeling O.K. now Mom.

Love to you and Sister--
James

October 5, 1945

Dear Folks,
Just a few words to tell you about the discharge. I took my papers up yesterday, notarized my letter, and handed the thing in. The board will meet on the 4th for consideration

of dependency discharges, and it will be at least the 18th or 20th before I will know anything on it. Perhaps, however, I'll have a much better birthday this year. Remember where I was a year ago? It just doesn't seem possible now that I was just out a couple of days from the island of Leyte.

Just wanted to keep you informed on proceedings. The fellow who took care of me said that 99% of such cases are being approved, but I could be in that other 1%, you know! If I should get out at the end of the month, I'm going to spend a couple of weeks with Dado and shoot me a deer or two!

All my love,
James

October 16, 1945

Dear Mother and Sister,
There is no word as yet on the results of my discharge request. Percy says that if it doesn't come through, he thinks I could be transferred to Balling Field and he could see that I get discharged from there. So perhaps I'll get home one of these days.

All my love,
James

And then . . .

Then came October 25, 1945, and we were processed and discharged! What a day! As always with the Army, there was much red tape, with the usual "go here, go there, hurry up and wait." But finally it was all done. And even with the absolute joy that the war was over and that we were on our way home, there was a sense of poignancy, too. We had shared an amazing adventure and now it was over. We were the lucky ones because we had survived. Too many of our friends had not. In looking back, I think our pride in what we had accomplished, and the special sense of comradeship we felt was perfectly illustrated by one of the last things we did. They lined us up in formation to march over to the post theater for the final ceremony. Off we marched, all in perfect order, everyone in step, making the movements with precision, heads held high. But there was a difference—THERE WAS NOBODY IN COMMAND! We were just doing it on our own! But we were old pros and mighty proud to be American soldiers!

Now What?

I was now a civilian trying to decide "Where do I go from here?" Fortunately I had the best help in the world. These included Dad's insurance friend from Abilene, Marvin Morrow; my uncle, Wilton Daniel, a bank president from Tyler; and my grandfather. The real question was, "What does James want to do with his life?" I could finish my interrupted education using the "GI Bill" or go into the insurance business. Because I wanted to come home and because I felt that mother needed me, I chose to enter the insurance agency full-time. We bought out dad's partner, Claude Crane and then sold a half-interest to a company friend of Morrow's, Edwin L. Stephens of Ft. Worth. He had seventeen years' experience with an insurance company.

This proved to be a marriage made in heaven for me. Steve became my best friend. He was the best insurance man I have ever met! He was Cherokee Indian originally from Tennessee, best man at my wedding, and took me to raise! He was married to Marie and had two high school–age daughters. We had a partnership for more than thirty-eight years that ended when he retired. The first three years of our partnership the two of us spent every night, every Saturday, and most Sunday afternoons at the office, which was my education in the specifics of the General Insurance Business. I also attended a six-week concentrated insurance course at the Maryland Casualty Insurance Company Headquarters in Baltimore, Maryland.

In November 1947, I married Mary Alice Bell. We had three children and enjoyed sixty-six years together until her death in 2014.

I joined the Midland Jaycees in about 1945 and made many lifetime friends there. Mary and I both taught Sunday School. I served a term on the City Council, am a Rotarian, and have served on numerous other boards, and organizations over the years. In due time, my son David quit his job as a federal bank examiner and joined the firm as a junior partner. So I had the pleasure of working with him for several years before my retirement in 1998. Mary and I have ten great-grandchildren.

In looking back, I am surprised at how much of my life has been shaped by the military, which was so much a part of my life for five formative years.

Index

INDEX